MW00934542

To ______________________

From ______________________

Previously published as *The Big Picture Interactive 52-Week Bible Story Devotional*

Written by Anna Sargeant

ISBN 978-1-5359-3497-8

Published by B&H Publishing Group
Nashville, Tennessee

Dewey Decimal Classification: C242.62
Subject Heading: DEVOTIONAL LITERATURE / BIBLE—STUDY AND TEACHING / CHRISTIAN LIFE

Printed in October 2020 in Heshan, Guangdong, China

3 4 5 6 7 8 24 23 22 21 20

ONE BIG STORY

52-WEEK BIBLE STORY DEVOTIONAL

Written by Anna Sargeant

Nashville, Tennessee

Features

The **One Big Story** brand is all about helping kids not only to know the Bible but also to know the God who has revealed Himself to us in its pages. Each week offers a devotion that ties to a Bible story along with pages of fun, thoughtful, and interactive features that can further connect kids with that week's message.

See page 224 for a Parent Connection, which is designed to empower parents to have a deeper conversation, in an age-appropriate way, with their kids. It's a great way to reinforce the content in this devotional and to inspire some great biblical insight for both parents and kids!

HEAR It!

Watch the full-page illustrations come alive using the free B&H Kids AR app. (Scan the QR code below to be taken to a page where you can download the Apple or Android version.) Just follow the instructions in the app—choose an icon, scan the illustration, and POP! Watch the Digital Pop-Ups™ jump off the page, and hear the short audio of the story.

Download the Free APP now!

Scan this QR code or search in the app store for "B&H Kids AR."

Then it's as easy as 1, 2, 3.

Tap any icon.

Scan the illustration.

Watch it come to life!

READ It!

We always love it when you go back to your Bible. Each devotion includes scripture references for you to look up so you can read more and learn more.

WATCH It!

Each story includes a QR code you can scan using any QR code reading app (including the B&H Kids AR app in QR mode). Scanning these QR codes will take you to a short video for that week's Bible story!

CHRIST Connection

Each devotion is based on a Bible story, and this helpful feature will show you how those stories point back to Christ and His work for us.

Putting your faith into action is important. This feature helps you do just that with great suggestions for living big and acting on each week's devotional message.

Perfect for family discussions, this list of questions will get you thinking and keep you talking.

Dear GOD,

Each prayer focuses on that week's content. Pray these words on your own, or pray them together as a family.

Contents

Old Testament Devotions

New Testament Devotions

Old Testament Devotions

Week 1

People Are Special

Have you ever looked up at a clear night sky? It's hard to count all the stars you see. Are there hundreds, thousands, millions perhaps? Scientists estimate that there are 300 billion stars in our galaxy alone. If you include the other 100 billion galaxies in the universe . . . well, God only knows how many stars there are! In fact, God knows how many stars there are *and* gives them each a name (Psalm 147:4).

But guess what? God knows way more about you than just your name! He knows the number of hairs on your head (Luke 12:7), the number of days in your life (Job 14:5), and everything you are doing throughout your day (Psalm 139). God knows all these facts about you *and* God also spends time thinking about you. The number of thoughts God has about you are more than the grains of sand on the seashore (Psalm 139:18). You are far more special than the stars.

Think back to creation, when God made the stars. God said, "Let there be lights in the sky," and boom! The sun, moon, and stars appeared. But when God made the first human, He said, "Let us make man in our own image," and Adam did not just appear. Instead of just speaking us into existence, God did something different. He took dust from the ground to make Adam's body, and He gave Adam life by breathing into his nostrils. Then God fashioned Eve out of one of Adam's ribs. Do you see? God *came close to us* in order to create us. He did this to show us how special we are.

From the very beginning, God has wanted to have a relationship with us. He wants us to talk to Him, listen to Him, and know Him. More than anything, God wants to show us His love. So the next time you look at a clear night sky, think about the One who created all those stars. Remember that very same God made you, knows you, thinks about you, and loves you. Remember that He thinks you are special.

HEAR It!

In the beginning, there was only God. He created the heavens and the earth and everything in them. Then God created man and woman in His own image. And God saw that His creation was good.

Week 1

READ It!

Psalm 139

Colossians 1:15-22

WATCH It!

CHRIST Connection

Colossians 1:15-22 reveals that Christ is ruler over all of God's creation. All of creation was created through Him, by Him, and for Him. Everything was created to give glory to Christ, but people would choose not to give Him glory. The rest of the Bible reveals how Jesus would restore the relationship between God and man.

This week, learn the names of five to ten stars. Try to find them in the night sky every night. As you look up at the stars, think about the God who loves you so much that He sent His very own Son to die for you. Thank Him for His love.

BIG PICTURE Questions

- What is your favorite thing God made in creation? Why is it your favorite?
- If you could ask God anything about what He made, what would you ask?
- Do you think God was there when Adam opened his eyes for the first time? Why or why not? What do you think Adam might have said or done when he first woke up?

Dear GOD,

Thank You for being a good creator of all. Thank You for showing us from the very beginning that we are special to You. When we look at the world around us, remind us of Your power and love. Thank You for sending Jesus, who made it possible for us to be close to You again.

Week 2

Listening to Lies

Have you ever believed what someone said, only to find out later it wasn't true? How did you feel when you found out you were believing a lie?

Did you know that the first time Adam and Eve sinned was when they believed a lie about God? Up until that point, Adam and Eve had always believed God's words and did what He said. But Satan got Adam and Eve thinking, "Is God *really* good? Can we believe *everything* He tells us?" God had said to Adam and Eve, "Do not eat from this tree. If you do, you will die." Then Satan declared, "You won't die. If you eat from this tree, you'll become like God."

Eve could have said, "Go away, Satan! I will not believe your lies." But Eve thought more and more about Satan's words. *To become like God*. That sounded pretty great. Soon Eve wanted to believe Satan more than she wanted to believe God. So she took the fruit and ate it, and Adam did too.

When we sin, we want something else more than we want God. Sin comes from believing lies instead of what God says.

Think about disobeying your parents. God says not to do it. Still, when your mom tells you to put away your laundry, you ignore her. You have better things to do! You have your own life to live! But when you disobey, you *still* have to put away your clothes, *and* you have to face the consequences of disobeying too. Sin is tricky like that. It promises something great that isn't true, and in the end, you are worse off.

This is why God sent Jesus to earth. Jesus came to do what no human could do. He came to resist Satan's lies and choose God every time. The Bible says Jesus was tempted to sin in every way but never sinned. This is why Jesus' death could pay for our sins! Jesus came because we believe the same lies Adam and Eve did, and we need someone else to keep God's law perfectly for us. With Jesus' help, we can learn to get better at saying, "Go away, Satan! I will not believe your lies."

HEAR It!

Adam and Eve didn't obey God, and this brought sin and sadness into the world. Sin is what keeps us apart from God. But God didn't leave us without hope—He sent His Son Jesus to save us from our sin.

Week 2

READ It!

Romans 5:18-19

2 Corinthians 5:21

WATCH It!

CHRIST Connection

Adam and Eve failed to give God glory when they introduced sin into the world, but God didn't leave them without hope. God sent His Son, Jesus, to live as Adam didn't—perfectly sinless. Jesus was God in the form of a man sent to rescue people from sin.

Eve believed Satan's lies and started to doubt that God was good. As you go through the week, write down ways God has been good to you. These could be prayers He has answered or gifts He has given. Remember that God is good all the time—sometimes we can see His goodness; sometimes we can't. When we do see God's goodness around us, let's stop and thank Him for it!

BiG PiCTURE Questions

- What are some things God says *not* to do? What are some things God does tell us to do?
- When you sin, do you get really upset with yourself? Remember, Jesus already died for that sin! When you sin, you can ask God for forgiveness and for help the next time you think about making the wrong choice.
- Do you ever wonder if God is good? Do you ever wonder if you can believe everything He tells you? When you wonder those things, talk to someone about it. God want you to wonder about Him and then believe the truth.

Dear GOD,

Thank You for sending Jesus, who did what we could not do and obeyed You every single time. Help us learn to say, "I will not believe lies about God." Help us to want You more than sin.

Week 3 When You Don't Understand

Angela was so excited her friend Rachel was coming over. Rachel's parents were missionaries, and she had only been in the US for a few weeks. When Rachel arrived, Angela led her to the kitchen, where the eggs, butter, flour, sugar, salt, baking powder, and vanilla extract were on the counter. "We're going to bake a cake!" Angela said.

Rachel glanced around, looking confused. "That turns into a cake?" she asked. Angela stopped to think. She supposed it was a strange idea. Butter, eggs, and white stuff transforming into a big, fluffy dessert. Angela turned to her friend. "It becomes a cake once we stick it in the oven. Trust me. It's deeeelicious!"

Noah probably felt like Rachel did when God told him to build an ark. Noah had never seen rain or a flood before. He did not know what an ark even was! Now God was telling him to build one so he and his family would be safe. At that point, Noah had a choice. He could tell God, "I have never seen rain or a flood. I don't understand what you're talking about, so I won't obey." Or Noah could listen to God, even though he didn't fully get it.

Have you ever been in a situation like Noah's? You know what God has said, but you don't get it? For example, God says that if someone wants to "take away your shirt, let him have your coat as well" (Matthew 5:40). Why would God ask us to do that? It seems like God would want you to keep your shirt and coat! It's hard to obey God when it doesn't make sense. How was Noah able to do it?

Noah had a relationship with God. God was his friend. God had never failed Noah before, so he could believe God now. Just like Rachel could trust Angela's words about the cake, Noah could trust God's words about the flood. God said the ark would save his family, so Noah knew it would, even though he didn't understand. By faith, Noah built the ark, and his family was saved!

HEAR It!

The people of the earth had become evil, and God was sorry He had made them. Only Noah obeyed God. God saved Noah and his family because Noah followed Him—just as God will save us, if we follow Him.

Week 3

READ It!

Proverbs 3:5-6

Hebrews 11:1, 7

WATCH It!

CHRIST Connection

The story of the flood shows us how serious God is about sin. He will not leave sin unpunished. But the story of Noah also shows us how loving God is. He provided a rescue plan for one righteous man—Noah. The rescue was extended to Noah's family. The story points ahead to a greater rescue! Jesus, the only perfectly righteous person, came to take the punishment for sin. We trust His act of obedience and are saved from the punishment our sin deserves.

When Noah built the ark, he had never even seen a boat. Noah had a lot to learn, so he listened to God's instructions. Try something this week that you've never tried before. Maybe it's a new game or a new skill. As you follow the instructions for learning something new, remember Noah, who trusted God and built an ark even when he didn't understand.

BIG PICTURE Questions

- Do you consider God to be your friend? Why or why not?
- Have you ever heard someone say something about God you didn't understand? What was it?
- Have you ever read something in the Bible that doesn't make sense? The next time you do, talk to your parents or teachers about it. God loves when His people study His Word together.

Dear GOD,

Thank You for the story of Noah, which shows us that You take sin seriously, but also that You provide a way for us to be saved! Thank You that Noah trusted You and built the ark even when he didn't completely understand. Help us always believe in You, even when we don't completely understand. Thank You for sending Jesus to save us from our sins.

Week 4

The Greatest Name

Mark held his breath as he waited along the fence. He watched as #13 warmed up with the catcher. Back and forth, back and forth, the ball whizzed through the air. It was the first time Mark had ever seen his favorite professional baseball player in person. Mark turned to his dad. "Do you think he'll give autographs?"

His dad smiled. "Sometimes athletes greet fans before the game, but sometimes there isn't time."

Mark groaned. "I really hope there's time! I want him to sign my ball, my glove, and my bat." After a short pause, Mark added, "And my cap! He's the greatest player who ever lived!"

Who is the most famous athlete you can think of living today? How about Singer? Actor? Scientist?

When God's people built the Tower of Babel long ago, they wanted to be famous too. God had told them to scatter themselves throughout the world so they could talk about His greatness and make *Him* famous. Instead, they built a tall tower so that everyone would look at them and think *they* were great.

The truth is Jesus is far greater than any person or group of people will ever be. He is the one who deserves everyone's worship. Philippians 2:10 promises that one day every knee will bow at the name of Jesus. That's because there is no one like Jesus! He is a perfect King who reigns over the whole universe, *and* He is a humble servant who came to die for sinners. But Jesus is not just great because of what He does. Jesus is great because of who He is—loving, forgiving, righteous, and faithful. Jesus will never let us down.

Is Mark's favorite baseball player awesome? No doubt. Is your favorite singer outstanding? For sure. God gives people incredible gifts and talents. As we stand amazed by these people, we can be even more in awe of the One who created them. And unlike our heroes, whose greatness fades, God's greatness lasts forever. He is far greater than anyone else—yesterday, today, and for all eternity.

HEAR It!

After the flood, God wanted the people to spread out and fill the earth again. But the people didn't do that! They gathered all together and began building a tower up to the skies. But God wasn't going to let His plan be stopped so easily!

Week 4

READ It!

Isaiah 12:4, Malachi 1:11, Philippians 2:5-11, Acts 4:12

WATCH It!

CHRIST Connection

Instead of glorifying God, people chose to ignore God's plan and glorify themselves. This didn't stop God's plan to scatter the people and to form nations. Eventually one of these nations would become God's chosen people. Through the nation of Israel, Christ would come to save the world.

Do some research about your favorite athlete, singer, actor, or scientist this week. What does their greatness teach you about God, their Creator?

- What does your name mean? Why did your parents give you your name?
- Jesus' name means "God saves." How does Jesus save us?
- List some ways that Jesus has been "great" in your family this year.

Dear GOD,

Thank You for showing us that You are far greater than anyone who has ever lived and Your name is the greatest name. There is no one like you. May we praise Your name in this family and tell others about the great things You have done for us.

Week 5

God's Great Promises

Think about a time you made a promise to someone. Did you keep that promise? Was it hard to keep? Now think about a time someone broke a promise to you. How did you feel? Is your relationship with that person different now?

Our God is a God who makes promises. In the book of Genesis, He made some pretty big promises to a man named Abram. God said, "I will make your name great. All the people of the earth will be blessed through you. And your offspring will be as many as the stars." Abram had great faith. He believed God's promises. We can look back now and see that every promise God made to Abram came true.

Did you know that the Bible is full of promises for those who believe in Jesus? God promises to send the Holy Spirit into our hearts so that we will never be alone (John 14:16). He promises to provide for all our needs (Philippians 4:19). He promises to help us resist every temptation (1 Corinthians 10:13). God promises that everything will work out for our good (Romans 8:28). And He promises that we will be forgiven of our sins and live forever with Him (John 3:16).

Sometimes it's hard to believe God's great promises. We think about the times others have broken their promises, and we think God will do the same thing. But God cannot lie. Everything that He says will happen does happen. But guess what? God kept His promises to Abram in a way Abram would have never expected. Out of Abram's family, God made a group of people, the Jews. Then through the Jews, God sent Jesus. So God blessed all the people of the world thousands of years after Abram lived, through Jesus! And remember how God promised He would make Abram's offspring as many as the stars? Those offspring are all the people who believe in Jesus!

The truth is we don't always know *how* God will keep His promises, but we can believe with confidence that He *will* keep them.

HEAR It!

God promised Abram that his offspring would be as many as the stars in the sky—even though Abram was an old man and had no children! But Abram believed God. He knew that nothing is impossible for God!

Week 5

READ It!

John 14:16, Philippians 4:19,
1 Corinthians 10:13,
Romans 8:28, John 3:16

WATCH It!

CHRIST Connection

God chose Abram to be the father of the nation in which Jesus would be born. In this way, Abram would bless all nations, as God had promised. God also saw Abram's faith in God's promises and counted it as righteousness. It is faith in Jesus' perfect righteousness that brings salvation to God's people.

Memorize one of the promises listed in the "Read It" section of this devotional. Recite this promise to a friend or family member. Write it on a piece of paper and display it in your room where you will see it often. When it seems like God might not be keeping that promise, remember that God kept His promise to Abram in a way Abram never expected!

BiG PiCTURE Questions

- When you sit in a chair, do you believe it will hold you up? What if you stood above the chair and kept saying "I believe it will hold me up" but never sat in it? Would you actually believe?
- Consider God's promise to never leave you alone. If you believed that promise all the time, how would your life be different?
- Consider God's promises to help us resist temptation. If you believed that promise all the time, what would you do when you were tempted to say something mean, for example?

Dear GOD,

Thank You for keeping Your promises to us. Help us believe them even when we don't know when or how You are going to keep them. Thank You for keeping Your promise to Abram and sending Jesus thousands of years later!

Week 6 Sacrifices and Substitutes

Imagine you got in so much trouble that you were sent to the principal's office. Now imagine just before you got there, the most obedient kid in class ran up to you and said "I'll go instead." Wow! Would you let him take your place? Would you let him take your punishment?

Throughout the Old Testament, God gave His people clues that Jesus would one day take our place. Sometimes these clues came through prophets like Isaiah, who said Jesus would be crushed for our wrongdoings. Sometimes these clues came through commands, like when God told the priest to make a sacrifice once a year for sin. And sometimes these clues happened as God interacted with people. Like the time God told Abraham to sacrifice his son Isaac.

That last example didn't seem to make sense! God had promised to keep His covenant to Abraham through Isaac's family. Now God was asking Abraham to take away Isaac's life? But Abraham trusted God even though he didn't understand. He obeyed God and prepared to sacrifice Isaac. Then God provided a ram as a substitute so Isaac could live.

God's interaction with Abraham was a huge clue about Jesus. Almost two thousand years after Isaac lived, God sent His Son, Jesus, to earth to die. But although God provided a ram to die in Isaac's place, nothing took Jesus' place. Jesus went to the cross even though He never sinned. He died in our place for our sin.

Think again about the most obedient kid offering to be punished instead of you. In that situation, you might face the principal yourself and deal with the consequences. But when it comes to God, the consequences are much greater. The Bible says the punishment for our sin is death, which includes living apart from God forever. We cannot fix this on our own. But more than two thousand years ago, Jesus came to fix it. When He died for us, Jesus proved how much God loves us. Now all we have to do is say, "Yes, I trust what Jesus has done. Jesus, take my place!"

HEAR It!

God wanted to be the most important thing in Abraham's life. So He asked Abraham to sacrifice his own son Isaac. Even though Abraham didn't understand, he was willing to obey God. God stopped Abraham and saved Isaac—just in time!

Week 6

READ It!

John 19:16-30

Romans 4:25

WATCH It!

CHRIST Connection

Abraham showed his faith in God when he was willing to sacrifice Isaac. Isaac also showed he was ready to do what his father said. This was a clear picture of God who was willing to sacrifice His only Son, and of Jesus who was willing to do what was necessary for God's plan of salvation. Isaac's life was spared because God provided a substitute. We need a perfect sacrifice as our substitute for sin. God provided a perfect sacrifice in His Son, Jesus.

God is still giving you clues about His love today. Look for them throughout the week. Look for them in the world around you, in your interactions with others, and in the Bible. Write down every clue you find, and share them with someone else.

BIG PICTURE Questions

- Have you ever had substitute teachers? How were they different from your real teacher? How were they the same? What does the word *substitute* mean?
- How is Jesus our substitute?
- Abraham didn't live long enough to see that his story was a clue about Jesus. Why do you think Abraham was able to trust God when he didn't understand?

Dear GOD,

Thank You for giving us all kinds of clues about Jesus in the Old Testament. It is sad to know that Jesus had to die to pay for our sins, but we are thankful He died and rose again. We trust You that this was the only way for our sins to be forgiven. Thank You for showing us how much You love us through Jesus.

Week 7

Life Is Not Fair

"Jamie, get in here!" her mother called from the playroom.

What's wrong? Jamie wondered, running down the hall. The moment she entered, she knew. Her art supplies were strewn all over the floor. And Jamie's little sister Marci sat in the corner, looking innocent.

"Why are your art supplies still out?" her mother demanded.
"I put them away earlier," Jamie promised. "It must have been Marci."

"Wasn't me!" Marci shouted. "I can't reach the shelf."

"I don't know how she did it," Jamie said. "But I know I put them away."

"Well, put them away again," her mother said before walking out the door.

Jamie cried, "Mom, that's not fair! It was Marci!" But her mother was already gone, and Jamie was left to clean up a mess that her little sister had made.

Has something like this ever happened to you? Maybe you were blamed for something you didn't do. Or someone else never got caught for something they did. Times like this make us want to pull our hair out! This is how Esau felt when Jacob stole his birthright. Jacob deceived his father and lied about it so he could receive Esau's blessing. Esau was so angry about this that he planned to kill Jacob. Although you might not want to kill the people who treat you unfairly, you probably get really upset about it, like Jamie in the story.

But imagine if Jamie had walked into the playroom, seen what Marci had done, and immediately started cleaning up the mess without complaining. Jesus did something far greater than that. He saw the sins we had committed, entered into our world, and chose to die for us. Was this fair? Not at all. It was far more unfair than anything we will ever face. But Jesus loved us so much, He did it. That means now, instead of focusing on everything that's unfair around us, we can focus on the gifts Jesus gives us—salvation from sins, an opportunity to know God, and peace, joy, and love that never end.

HEAR It!

God had a plan to bless Jacob's life. But Jacob tried to get that blessing by lying, stealing, and tricking. Because of this, Jacob had to leave his home and family and travel to a faraway land. Nothing good comes from lying, stealing, or tricking.

Week 7

Psalm 73:2-5, 26-28

1 Peter 3:18

CHRIST Connection

Jacob is a perfect example of why a Savior was needed. Like Jacob, we seek a birthright and blessing that is not ours, but we cannot lie, deceive, or trick to receive it. Instead Jesus shared His birthright and blessing with us when He paid for our sins on the cross and gave us His righteousness.

Pretend you're a reporter, and interview your parents. Ask them to tell you about a time when they were treated unfairly but things turned out okay in the end. Remember to ask for the details: age, time, place, events. Why were they okay with the outcome? Did their faith in God grow because of the situation?

BIG PICTURE Questions

- Describe a recent time something unfair happened to you. Has something unfair ever turned out to be good for you?
- What do you usually do when life is unfair and no one seems to be listening to you?
- Who is always listening to us?

Dear GOD,

Thank You for telling us about Jacob and Esau and the way their story shows us our need for You through Jacob's actions and Esau's reaction. Jacob had to lie and cheat to earn his blessing, but we can receive so many blessings freely in Jesus simply through faith in Him. Thank You for sending Jesus to be treated unfairly for us.

Week 8

God Is Always Good

Imagine you are a baby bird. You are nestled safely next to your brothers and sisters in your nice house made of twigs. Every day, your parents bring you fat, juicy worms. Yummy! Life is good. It involves eating, chirping, and watching the world around you. Little do you know there is something wonderful missing—flying.

Did you know that some baby birds refuse to leave their nest and learn to fly? When that happens, the mother bird often stands on a tree branch with the food so the baby has to leave the nest to grab it. If that doesn't work, the mother will even push her baby out of the nest! Can you imagine being that baby bird, tumbling through the air, trying to use your new wings, not knowing what is happening? Those baby birds probably wonder, *Why is my mother doing this to me?* But we know why. The baby needs to learn to fly. Flying, after all, is what birds are made to do.

Joseph might have wondered, *Why is God doing this to me?* during his life. In the beginning, everything seemed great. He was his father's favorite. He had a fancy coat. And he had dreams of his brothers bowing down to him. But soon, things took a turn for the worse. His brothers sold him into slavery. He was unfairly sent to jail. And his friends forgot about him. Even though Joseph lived through scary times, God was still with him. Like a bird mother preparing her babies for flight, God was preparing Joseph for the day he would lead Egypt.

Life is confusing and scary for us at times too. Sometimes loved ones get sick and even die. Sometimes school is harder than we expect. Sometimes we have to move, or a good friend moves away. But God is good even when life is scary. Romans 8:28 tells us God works *all things* out for the good of those who love Him. You can trust that promise right now and in the scary times to come.

HEAR It!

Joseph was attacked by his own brothers. He was sold into slavery, lied about, and then thrown into jail! But God was always with him. He blessed him, even in hard times. God never left Joseph—and He will never leave you!

Week 8

READ It!

Isaiah 12:2, Genesis 50:20, Romans 8:28

CHRIST Connection

God sent Joseph to Egypt and blessed him, so that he rose to a position of great power. In that position, he was God's instrument for saving his family and many others in the world from death by starvation. Jesus gave up His position of great power to be God's instrument for saving people. Christ's life and death made a way to save people from spiritual death, which is the penalty of sin.

Draw a picture of something that has happened to you that was scary. Now draw a picture of something you are afraid *will* happen to you in the future. Cut out a large cross and glue it onto the picture. Remember, it was hard for Jesus to die for our sins, but He did anyway because He loves you. No scary thing is more powerful than Jesus' love for you.

BIG PICTURE Questions

- Talk about a time recently when you felt scared or confused.
- Talk about a time something good took a turn for the worse.
- Have you ever wondered *Why is God doing this to me?* If you haven't, you probably will someday. What can you remember when that question comes to mind?

Dear GOD,

Thank You for the story of Joseph, which reminds us that You are always with us. When life is hard or scary, help us remember You are working all things out for our good. Thank You for sending Jesus to do a scary thing and die for our sins so we can know You.

Week 9

God Is Always Right

Are you ever tempted to think that God is wrong? Well, you probably would never say the words "God is wrong," but maybe you think, *God doesn't mean exactly what He says*. For example, even though God says "Do not lie," you might think, *God would be okay with this little white lie, because He loves me and wouldn't want me to get in trouble. So . . . I guess I know what God really means. He means it's only wrong to tell big lies*. When we change what God says, it's like we are saying He is wrong. But God is never wrong.

God says exactly what He means and means exactly what He says. When God gives a command, He means to. When God says something will happen, it will. Joseph and his brothers found that out thousands of years ago. When Joseph was a boy, God gave him dreams of his brothers bowing down to him. When Joseph told his brothers about the dreams, they got pretty upset. In fact, they were so mad they sold Joseph into slavery! They probably thought, *There's no way those dreams will come true now!*

But when God says something will happen, it will. Sure enough, years later, Joseph's brothers came to Egypt to buy grain during the famine. Because Joseph had been put in charge of all of Egypt, his brothers bowed down to him, just as God said they would.

The words in the Bible are not there by accident. God meant to say them. He meant for us to hear the stories, listen to the commands, and believe the promises. So the next time you are tempted to think, *God must have meant something else*, remember the story of Joseph and his brothers. Remember that what God says is true. Always.

HEAR It!

Joseph had once dreamed that his brothers would bow before him—and now that dream had come true! Though his brothers had tried to harm Joseph, God used their evil plans to do a great good. Many lives were saved—even the lives of his brothers!

Week 9

READ It!

Numbers 23:19

Proverbs 30:5

Matthew 24:35

WATCH It!

CHRIST Connection

Joseph recognized that though his brothers intended evil, God planned his circumstances for good—to establish a remnant of God's people (Genesis 45:7). Likewise, though those who crucified Jesus intended it for evil, God's plan for the sacrifice of His Son was for the good of all people. Through Jesus' death on the cross, God again saved a remnant of people.

Play the opposite game with a friend or family member. *How to play*: Say the exact opposite of what you mean, back and forth to each other. For example, if you want pancakes for breakfast, say, "I don't want pancakes for breakfast." When you play, remember that God doesn't play the opposite game. He always means exactly what He says and says exactly what He means.

BiG PiCTURE Questions

- When was the last time you were wrong about something? Maybe it was on a test at school, or you thought something that wasn't true about a friend? Are you okay with being wrong? Why or why not?
- It's great to know that God is never wrong. But how does that affect your life today? How can your life change because that is true?

Dear GOD,

Thank You for the story of Joseph, which reminds us that You had a plan to save Your people from the very beginning. You are always right. You were right about the past, You are right about today, and You are right about the future. You tell us that one day Jesus will come back, and we trust that is true. Help us to live like we believe it.

Week 10

Excuses, Excuses

James had one job this weekend—to take out the trash. There was just one problem. James *hated* taking out the trash. First of all, trash is smelly. Second of all, there were nine trash cans in James's house—two in the kitchen, two in the bathrooms, one in each bedroom, and one in the garage. Plus James's house was a two-story house. That meant lots of trips to grab all the trashcans. Taking out the trash was no small job! Besides, James had better things to do. There were neighbors to hang out with and school projects to finish. And it's not like the trash was going anywhere. . . .

Have you ever found yourself making excuses for your disobedience? James's parents gave him one chore, and he came up with plenty of reasons for not doing it. This is the same attitude Moses had when God told him to lead His people out of Egypt. Moses did not like what God was asking him to do, so he thought of reasons why he shouldn't. He told God the people wouldn't believe him and that he was not good with words. These excuses revealed what was going on in Moses' heart. Moses did not trust God enough to obey Him. In the end, God sent Moses' brother Aaron to Egypt with Moses, because Moses would not go on his own.

We are all quick to come up with reasons why we should not obey God. For example, when God says to love our enemies we say, "I've tried to love so-and-so before, but she's still mean to me. So I'm going to stop." The truth is, God tells us to do what seems impossible *so that* we will rely on Him for help. So the next time you're tempted to make an excuse to disobey, ask God for help instead. Watch what happens when you do!

HEAR It!

God had a plan for Moses' life. He saved the baby Moses from the Nile River, and He saved Moses from Pharaoh's anger. At the burning bush, God shared His plan with Moses. If Moses would only trust God, the Hebrew people would be saved!

Week 10

READ It!

James 1:13-15

Romans 2:4

WATCH It!

CHRIST Connection

God saved Moses for a special purpose: to rescue His people. The calling of Moses points to a great calling and rescue—the call of Jesus to come to earth to save God's people from their sin. Moses and Jesus both obeyed God's commands in order to carry out His plan of salvation. Moses delivered God's people from physical captivity; Jesus delivered God's people from captivity to sin.

Write down which of God's commands is hardest for you to obey right now. Ask God to help you obey that command this week. If you still disobey, remember, God forgives. If you obey, praise God for helping you!

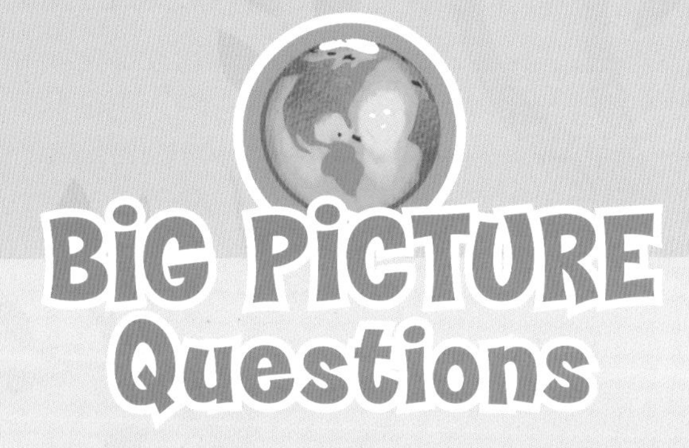

BIG PICTURE Questions

- Have you ever felt like James? Like you have all the reasons in the world *not* to do what you've been told? When was that?
- Why do you think Moses didn't want to go to Egypt? (Think about what God was asking him to do.) Moses was afraid. Would you have been afraid?

Dear GOD,

Thank You for giving us this story to remind us that Your commands will be too hard to obey without Your help. Forgive us when we make up excuses for our disobedience, and thank You for giving us all the help we need.

Week 11

Warning, Warning!

There are warnings all around us to keep us from harming ourselves. God gives us warnings in nature, like the rattling of a snake's tail or the heat from a fire's flame. Man-made warnings are helpful too, like yellow traffic lights and No Diving! signs. Warnings are good for us. They make us aware of danger and protect us from the consequences of unwise choices.

Pharaoh, the king of Egypt, did not pay attention to God's warnings. Every time God sent a plague to Egypt, He warned Pharaoh beforehand. But Pharaoh would not listen. Why not? If God told Pharaoh exactly what was going to happen, why did Pharaoh ignore Him?

Do you ever ignore the warnings around you? Do you run at the pool when you've been warned you might slip? Do you keep talking in class when you've been warned you'll lose time at recess? You and I ignore warnings because we'd rather do what we feel like doing. We want to make up our own rules.

Pharaoh spent most of his life doing what he wanted and making up his own rules. The Egyptians even believed Pharaoh was a god, and they worshiped him like he was one. Then along came Moses saying Pharaoh was not a god at all and there was one true God who deserved to be worshiped! This one true God demanded that Pharaoh release the people from slavery so they could go worship *Him*. Pharaoh did not let the people go because he did not want to face the truth: there was only one God in the universe who had power to send plagues and who truly deserved to be worshiped.

We can sometimes have a heart like Pharaoh. We ignore warnings about sin. We would rather make up our own rules. But God gives us warnings about sin because He is the one true God who knows what is best for us. So the next time you are tempted to ignore God, ask Him for faith to listen to the warning and obey.

HEAR It!

Pharaoh's heart was hard. He would not let God's people go. God sent plague after plague against the Egyptian people, but still Pharaoh would not listen. There was one more plague to come, and it would be the most terrible one of all!

Week 11

READ It!

Zechariah 7:8-11

Ezekiel 36:26

2 Corinthians 5:17

WATCH It!

CHRIST Connection

God called Moses to be His servant. He was a great servant who obeyed God and led the Israelites out of slavery. The Bible says that Jesus is greater than Moses (Hebrews 3:3). Jesus was a servant who obeyed God perfectly and suffered to free His people from sin.

With your parents, read the warning labels on medicine bottles and cleaning supplies around the house. What do the warning labels look like? Do they catch your attention? What might happen to someone who did not listen to those warnings?

BIG PICTURE Questions

- Recall a time you ignored a warning. Why did you ignore it? What happened?
- Do you think you've ignored more than ten warnings in your life? Are you surprised Pharaoh ignored God ten times in a row?
- What warnings do you want to start paying more attention to?

Dear GOD,

Thank You for giving us warnings about sin and showing us the best way to live. Forgive us when we ignore Your warnings as Pharaoh did and make up our own rules. Help us listen to You and obey You. Thank You that Jesus obeyed perfectly so that He was a perfect sacrifice for our sins.

Week 12

God Makes Us Free

Markus sat in prison next to his team's flag. He watched as his teammates entered the enemy's territory, either to head back to safety or be tagged themselves. Suddenly, from the corner of the field, Jess made a break for it. "Come on, Jess!" Markus and the other prisoners shouted. They was eager to be released, eager to play again. Soon Jess was five steps away. Then three steps. Now one. Markus reached out his hand for Jess to tag. *Slap*. Jess had set them free! They could all play capture the flag again!

The Israelites were in a much worse situation than Markus was in capture the flag. The Israelites had been slaves in Egypt for 430 years. As slaves, they worked hard for wicked masters who treated them poorly, and they were not allowed to worship God. For a long time, they cried out to God to save them and waited for His answer.

Think about how hard it is to be a slave. You must always do what your master says. If you say no, a wicked master might whip you or take away your food. Think about Markus in the capture-the-flag prison. He wasn't allowed to leave. When people are prisoners or slaves, their master is in total control.

Did you know the Bible tells us that we are slaves to sin? Without God's help, we are controlled by it. We need God to set us free!

For the Israelites, Passover was a special night because God set them free from slavery in Egypt. But Passover was also one of God's big clues about Jesus. On Passover night, the firstborn sons of those who sacrificed a spotless lamb did not have to die. Thousands of years later, Jesus died on the cross as a sacrifice for our sins. Today those who trust in Jesus do not face the punishment of eternal death. That means we have been set free too! Free to worship and obey God—today, tomorrow, and forever.

HEAR It!

God was going to send a terrible plague as a judgment against all of Egypt. But God had a plan to save His people, the Israelites. The blood of a lamb sprinkled on their doorposts would let God know to "pass over" their homes.

Week 12

Luke 4:16-21

Romans 6:6, 22

CHRIST Connection

By His grace, God spared the Israelites from judgment by requiring the blood of a lamb. Jesus is the Lamb of God, who takes away the sin of the world. His death was the ultimate sacrifice, and those who trust in Christ are under His saving blood and will be passed over in the final judgment.

Hang a red ribbon somewhere in your house. Anyone who sees the red ribbon has to recite John 1:29, "John saw Jesus coming toward him and said, 'Here is the Lamb of God, who takes away the sin of the world!'" Once everyone in the family has recited the verse at least once, take down the ribbon and hang it from a new place the next morning. Keep moving the ribbon and reciting the verse throughout the week.

BiG PiCTURE Questions

- Do you think the Israelites were surprised by how God set them free from slavery in Egypt?
- Are you surprised that the way God frees us from sin is to trust in Jesus' sacrifice?
- What is one sin you wish you could easily resist? Ask God to help you resist that temptation this week.

Dear GOD,

Thank You for setting Your people free from slavery all those years ago. Thank You for giving us a clue, even back them, about how You would set us free through Jesus' death on the cross. Thank You that sin does not control us anymore and that we are free to serve You and worship You.

Week 13 From Grumbling to Gratitude

Toby hopped in the car after school. "How about an ice cream cone?" his dad asked.

Toby smiled. "Woohoo!" After ice cream, Toby's dad took him to the video game store so Toby could try the hottest new release. Then he dropped Toby off at Seth's house while he ran a few more errands.

"This is the best day ever!" Toby said as he and Seth shot basketballs.

An hour later, Toby's dad returned. "Time to go," he said.

"Just a couple more!" Toby answered. "I've made seven in a row!"

"Your mom called and said dinner is ready. We need to leave now."

Toby's shot bounced off the side of the rim. "Look what you made me do, Dad!" he whined.

His dad's voice was stern. "Son, put down the basketball."

Toby slammed the basketball into the ground. "You never let me have any fun!" he shouted. His dad didn't say a word. Toby looked at his feet. "Well, that's not totally true," he said. "We did do a lot of fun things today."

"You're right," his dad said. "And eating dinner might not be fun, but it is good for us."

Toby nodded and handed the ball to Seth. As they walked out together, he said, "Thanks for everything, Dad."

Have you ever had a reaction like Toby's? You didn't get your way, so you whined about it, even though there was still much to be thankful for?

Consider the Israelites. God delivered them from slavery and then parted the Red Sea so they could escape their enemies. For a while, everything was great, but soon they couldn't find water or food. They complained to God, saying, "You brought us out here to die!" But that wasn't true. God loved the Israelites and provided them with everything they needed.

You and I won't always get our way. When we don't, we'll be tempted to complain just like the Israelites. Focusing on God's goodness will help change our grumbling into gratitude. Remembering that God always does what's best will remind us to be thankful, whether we are getting our way or not.

HEAR It!

The Israelites were trapped! The Egyptians were on one side and the Red Sea was on the other. But God was going to fight for His people. The sea parted, and the Israelites walked across on dry ground. When the Egyptians followed, the waters came crashing back!

Week 13

Deuteronomy 6:20-23, Psalm 42:1-5, Psalm 77:11

CHRIST Connection

God created a way for the Israelites to escape the Egyptians. In the same way, God planned the way for people to escape the penalty of sin. God's Son, Jesus, is the only way to get to God.

Write down the last time you didn't get your way. Write down the name of the person who kept you from getting your way. Now write down three times that person has shown you that he or she loves you. How can you change your grumbling to gratitude?

This week, remember that God's love is perfect and far greater than any human's love. He is a good God who always does what is best for us.

- What does it feel like when you don't get your way?
- What do you think the Israelites thought when they couldn't find food or water? What do you think they thought when God provided what they needed?
- Talk about why God might not always let us get our way. What might He be teaching us?

Dear GOD,

Thank You for saving us even when we didn't deserve it. Help us remember what You are truly like when we begin to doubt Your goodness. Help us to trust that You want what's best for us and love us. Thank You for giving us Jesus.

Week 14

A Rule for a Reason

Madison looked at the clock. It was almost time for Amy's pool party! Madison loved that pool. It had a water slide and a volleyball net. Plus, there were plenty of pool toys.

"Maddie, let's go!" her mom called. Madison looked inside her bag. Flipflops. *Check*. Towel. *Check*. Sunglasses. *Check*. Sunscreen. *Not here*. This was one of the family rules: Always wear sunscreen while swimming. But Madison didn't want to look for it.

"Coming, Mom!" she called, taking two stairs at a time. *I don't HAVE to wear sunscreen*, Madison thought. *It's not THAT important*.

That evening, when Madison's mom picked her up, she gasped. "You're completely sunburned!"

Madison looked down at her arms. They were bright red. *I guess that's a rule for a reason*, Madison thought.

Rules. They are everywhere. On the playground, in our classrooms, on the roads. Rules exist to keep us safe. Think about some rules you are told to keep. Which is the hardest one to follow?

Thousands of years ago, God gave His people ten rules called the Ten Commandments. The first four rules were about loving God. The last six rules were about loving people. These rules showed the people how they could worship God. Obeying these rules was also the best thing for the people. Think about Madison's mom. She made the "Always wear sunscreen" rule because she knew their family's skin burned easily. God's rules also exist to protect us. When God said, "Do not be jealous of your neighbor's things," He knew jealousy would destroy our relationships.

Ultimately, God's rules help us the most by showing us how much we need Jesus, who came to earth to do what we could never do—follow all of God's rules perfectly. God gave us Jesus because He loves us. Once we trust in Jesus, we're not trying to keep the rules so God will love us; we can keep the rules because we know for sure we are already loved.

HEAR It!

God spoke to Moses on the mountaintop and gave him the Ten Commandments. These were God's rules for how to live a holy life. But while Moses was with God, the Israelites began to worship a golden calf! They were already breaking God's rules.

Week 14

READ It!

Exodus 20:1-17, Matthew 5:17, John 14:15

WATCH It!

CHRIST Connection

God made a covenant with His people. "If you obey Me, you will be my people" (Exodus 19:5-6). But the people did not obey God. They sinned against God, and Moses asked God to forgive them. Moses acted as their mediator, or advocate, before God. When we sin, Jesus is our mediator. Through Jesus, we are forgiven of our sins. God is pleased with us because He looks at Jesus, who never sinned.

Draw a picture of yourself obeying a rule that you think is hard to obey. Do you know God will still love you the same, even though you don't always obey this rule? That's right—God's love does not change based on what we do or don't do! But God knows that rules are good for us, so He wants us to obey. The next time you have a hard time obeying the rule you drew, ask God for help.

- Imagine a day with no rules! What would it be like to have no rules in your classroom? In your cafeteria? On your playground? In what ways would no rules be awesome? In what ways would no rules be terrible?
- Jesus came to earth and obeyed every single one of God's rules. Keeping that in mind, do you think God's rules matter?
- What's the difference between trying to keep the rules to earn God's love, and keeping the rules because you are already loved?

Dear GOD,

Thank You for giving us rules to show us how to worship You. Even if we wanted to, we know we could never obey every rule You gave because we are sinners. Thank You for sending Jesus to obey every rule we could never obey. Thank You for seeing Him when you look at us.

Week 15 Using Our Mouths for Good

When God made the human body, He certainly thought things through. Consider your mouth. It's a pretty busy part of the body. We breathe through it, eat with it, and talk with it. Here are some fun facts about the mouth:

- Your tongue is the strongest muscle in your body, considering its size.
- Everyone has a unique tongue print, just like we all have a unique fingerprint.
- Our teeth are actually bones, with blood and nerves running through them.
- Kids have twenty teeth. By the time they are grown-ups, they have thirty-two.

Because God made our mouths, He can use them to bring Himself glory. In the story of Balaam, God used the mouths of His creatures to show His power. First God spoke to Balaam through his donkey. Then God spoke through Balaam to the king of Moab, the enemy of the Israelites. Three times Balaam said, "I can only say what God tells me." Then Balaam blessed God's people, said true things about God, and prophesied about the future, including prophesying about Jesus.

When Jesus came to earth, He was a perfect prophet. This means He delivered God's message exactly how God wanted. Remember how Balaam said, "I can only say what God tells me"? Well, Jesus said something even more amazing: "I have not spoken on My own, but the Father Himself who sent Me has given Me a command as to what I should say and what I should speak" (John 12:49). And one the most important things Jesus said was that He had come to save sinners.

God still works powerfully through the mouths of His people. When we tell the truth, talk to others about Jesus, and encourage one another, we are like light, pushing back the darkness around us. God says each of us has a choice—we can use our mouths to honor Him and bless others, or we can use our mouths to dishonor him and hurt others. God wants to help us use our mouths to honor Him. How will you use your mouth today?

HEAR It!

Balaam, a sorcerer, was on his way to see the king of Moab. Three times the angel of the Lord stopped his donkey, and three times Balaam hit the donkey. Then the donkey spoke! "Why are you hitting me?" That's when Balaam knew he should listen to the Lord God.

Week 15

READ It!

Psalm 22:22, Proverbs 13:3, James 3:1-12

CHRIST Connection

Fourteen hundred years after Balaam announced Jesus' birth, wise men followed a star to the place where Jesus was born. The wise men worshiped Jesus as King (Matthew 2:2).

Study your mouth in the mirror. What do you notice about the top of your tongue? What about the bottom of your tongue? Try to count your teeth. Are there any missing? What does the back of your throat look like? After you have studied your mouth, say something true about God aloud. Thank Him for all the wonderful things your mouth can do.

BIG PICTURE Questions

- Animals don't typically talk. What do you think you would have done if you had heard a donkey speak?
- Think about the last time you used your mouth to help people. How did they respond? Even if people don't respond well to your words, remember: God gets glory when you use your mouth for good.
- Think about the last time you used your mouth to hurt someone. What happened? Did you ever apologize?

Dear GOD,

Thank You for giving us mouths for breathing, eating, and talking. Help us to honor You with our mouths through truthful and good words. Remind us that there is power in the name of Jesus, so when we talk about Jesus, we don't have to be afraid. Thank You for sending Jesus to deliver Your message of hope for sinners.

Week 16 Surprised by God's Plans

Imagine you go for a hike in the woods and you suddenly see a bear on the path in front of you. What should you do? Should you get out of there as fast as you can? Should you stand still and stay silent? Experts say no to both. If a bear spots you, you are supposed to use a calm voice and speak to it. That's right—talk to the bear! On top of that, you should wave your arms. Yes, it seems as if you're asking the bear to come and eat you! This advice is surprising and goes against common sense. But the fact is, doing these things helps the bear figure out you are a human and won't hurt the bear.

God's plan for taking the city of Jericho must have been surprising to Joshua. It went against common sense. Joshua had an army of men who were ready to fight. Marching around a wall, sounding trumpets, and shouting was not a good military strategy. But God told Joshua why it would work: after the people obeyed God's instructions, God Himself would make the walls of Jericho fall down. Then the Israelites could rush in and take the city. God's strange plan would lead to their victory.

The Bible tells us of other times when God's plans were surprising. When Jesus was on earth, He surprised the people around him. He hung out with thieves and lawbreakers, and He turned fishermen into disciples. But Jesus' death on the cross was the most surprising of all. This was all part of God's plan—for Jesus to die for sinners. Many people do not accept this plan. It goes against common sense! They want to be able to get to God on their own. But God says no one can be good enough to save themselves. There is one way to be saved: turn from your sins and believe in Jesus. If this surprises you, that's okay. God's love is too grand for us to understand. But God's love is real, and it's there for you. You can know it when you trust in Jesus.

HEAR It!

Joshua sent two spies to the city of Jericho. When the king's men came looking for the spies, a woman named Rahab hid them. She knew that their God was the one true God—and she knew that He was her only hope of getting out of Jericho alive.

Week 16

READ It!

1 Corinthians 1:18-25
Romans 3:9-11
Ephesians 3:18-21

WATCH It!

CHRIST Connection

God gave the city of Jericho to the Israelites. He fought the battle for them and told them not to take anything from the city. God promised to provide for His people's needs. Jesus spoke of God's provision in Matthew 6:33, "Seek first the kingdom of God and His righteousness, and all these things will be provided for you." Jesus meets our greatest need—to be saved from sin. We can trust Him for our salvation.

Write down one or two ways you could show surprising love to someone this week. Now challenge yourself to do so before the end of the week.

BIG PICTURE Questions

- Name one loving thing someone did for you recently. Was it surprising at all? If it wasn't surprising, try to think of a time someone did show you love in a surprising way. How did that make you feel?
- If you could come up with your own way to get to heaven, what would it be?
- How does your get-to-heaven plan compare with God's plan? Remember that God's plan is the only way anyone can be saved. Thank God for His plan of salvation.

Dear GOD,

You show us through the story of the conquest of Jericho that You are the One who wins the battles for us. You might not fight in the way we expect, but there is always a victory with You. Thank You for sending Jesus so we can be saved from sin. Thank You for Your surprising love.

Week 17

God Always Wins

Dr. Martin Luther King Jr. was a civil rights leader in the United States during the 1950s and '60s. He, along with many of his friends, fought for African-American citizens to have the same rights as white citizens. This struggle was not easy. Dr. King was beaten, arrested, and sent to jail many times. After one of those arrests, Dr. King was put in a dark prison cell with no bed. While in that lonely room, he wrote a letter to white leaders in America. The letter was later published by many newspapers and read by thousands. It changed the way many people thought about African-American rights in the country. The men who threw Dr. King into the Birmingham jail thought they were silencing him. Little did they know what would happen in that prison cell. Little did they know the change that would come because of the letter.

Now think about the story of Samson. The Philistines were probably so relieved after they cut off Samson's hair. *The hair gave him his strength! Now he can never harm us again!* they must have thought. Little did they know God was the real source of Samson's strength. So when Samson cried out to God, "Strengthen me once more," God did. Samson brought down the temple of the Philistines' false god, and God's people were saved.

Sometimes we think, *Evil is winning! Where is God?* The Bible tells us exactly where He is. God is always up to something good, even when evil forces are working hard to get in God's way. Think about Jesus dying on the cross. The Jewish leaders thought they were getting rid of Jesus by killing Him. Little did they know that God was working behind the scenes, saving us from our sins. Three days later, Jesus proved this was true when He rose from the dead and walked out of the tomb.

Even when it looks like evil is winning, God will always triumph. You can put your hope in Him. He is always up to something good, even if it is behind the scenes.

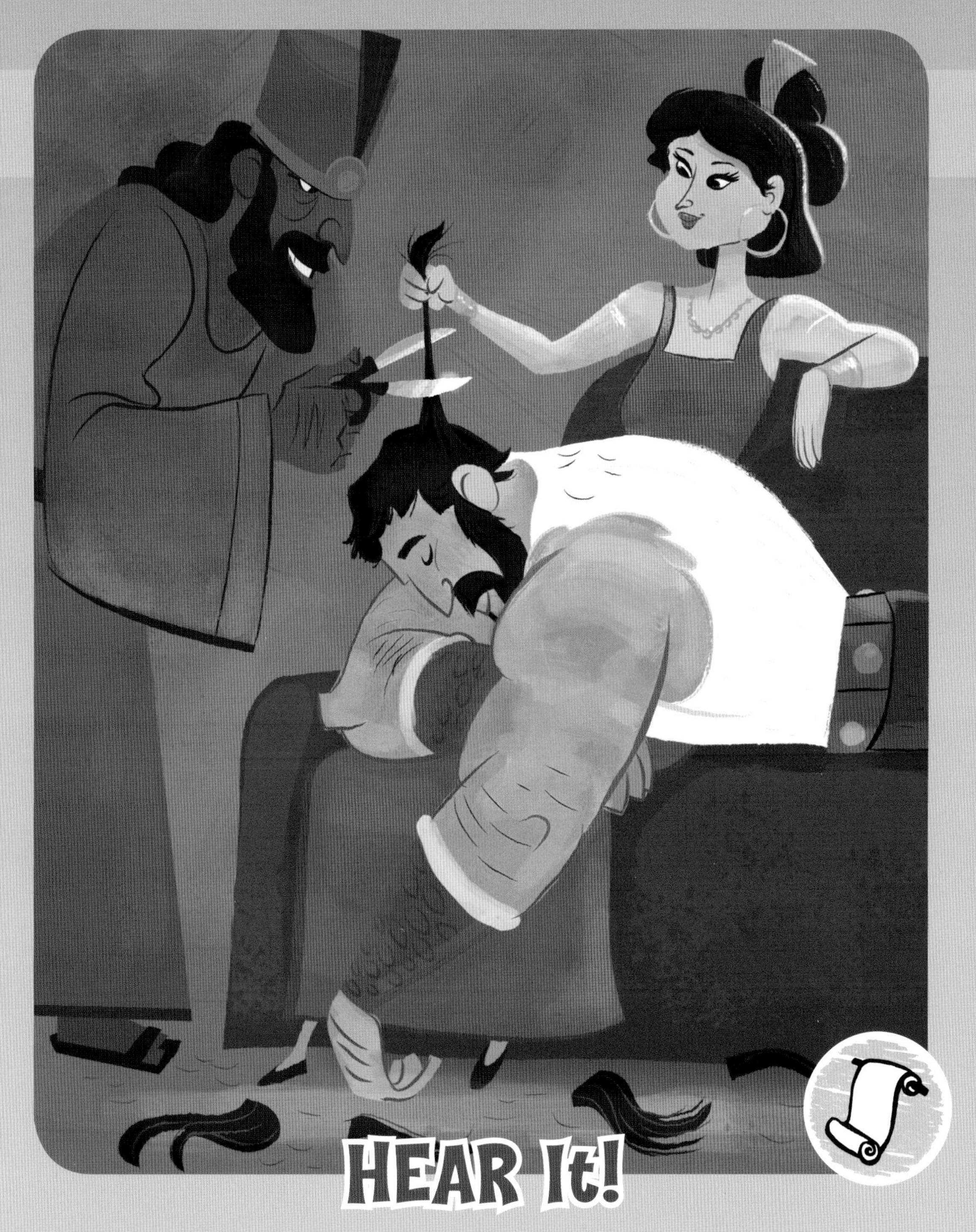

HEAR It!

God blessed Samson with great strength—as long as he never cut his hair. Samson defeated many Philistines. But when he fell in love with Delilah, a Philistine woman, she told his enemies the secret of his strength. Samson was captured, but God gave him great strength one last time!

Week 17

READ It!

Psalm 10:1-7, 12-15

Acts 2:22-24

WATCH It!

CHRIST Connection

God raised up Samson as the last judge to deliver the Israelites from the Philistines. Samson killed more Philistines in his death than he did in his life. Jesus would come as the last Deliverer, saving through His life and His death those who would trust in Him.

Play a board game this week. On every turn, each player needs to write down if he thinks he is going to win or lose. At the end, look at the winning player's record. How many times did it look like the winner was losing? Remember that God always wins, even when it looks like He is losing.

BIG PICTURE Questions

- Is there something in your life right now you wish you could change? Do you feel like if it changed, everything would be better?
- What did Martin Luther King Jr. and Samson do when their enemies captured them? Did they give up?
- What can you do when life gets hard?

Dear GOD,

You always win. Even when it looks like evil is silencing You, You are at work behind the scenes. You will cause all things to work out for Your glory and our good. Help us to never lose our faith or trust in You. We put our hope in only You.

Week 18

All People Are Important

Monique awoke with a jolt. Today was her first day of fourth grade. Well, technically, this was her third time for a first day of fourth grade. It was only February, and Monique had already been in two other schools this year. Her father moved a lot for work.

Monique slid out of bed, the butterflies dancing around in the stomach. She wondered about her new school. *Will I like my teacher? Will I make any friends?* Monique shuffled to the kitchen to eat her breakfast. *I just hope it's better than my last school*, she thought.

Have you ever been the new kid in school? It's hard to be the new kid anywhere. There's so much you don't know and so much to learn. You hope at least one person will be nice to you.

Ruth probably felt that way when she came to Bethlehem. She was from another country. She was a widow, which means her husband had died, and she was very poor. Ruth knew only one person, her mother-in-law, Naomi. But God had a plan to take care of Ruth. There was a man named Boaz living in Bethlehem. He was a man of God and Naomi's family redeemer. He kept Ruth safe and made sure she had enough food. When the time was right, Boaz married Ruth so he could take care of her completely. And guess what? Ruth became the great, great, great, great . . . great-grandmother of Jesus!

Through the story of Ruth, God shows us how much He cares about outsiders. God stands up for those who feel left out—people like the poor, the sick, and the neglected. When Jesus came to earth, He spent a lot of time with these kinds of people. This proved that God's love is not only for people the world sees as important. God gladly pays attention to the people nobody else does because all people have equal value in God's eyes. With God's help, we can see everyone the way He does and love them with His love.

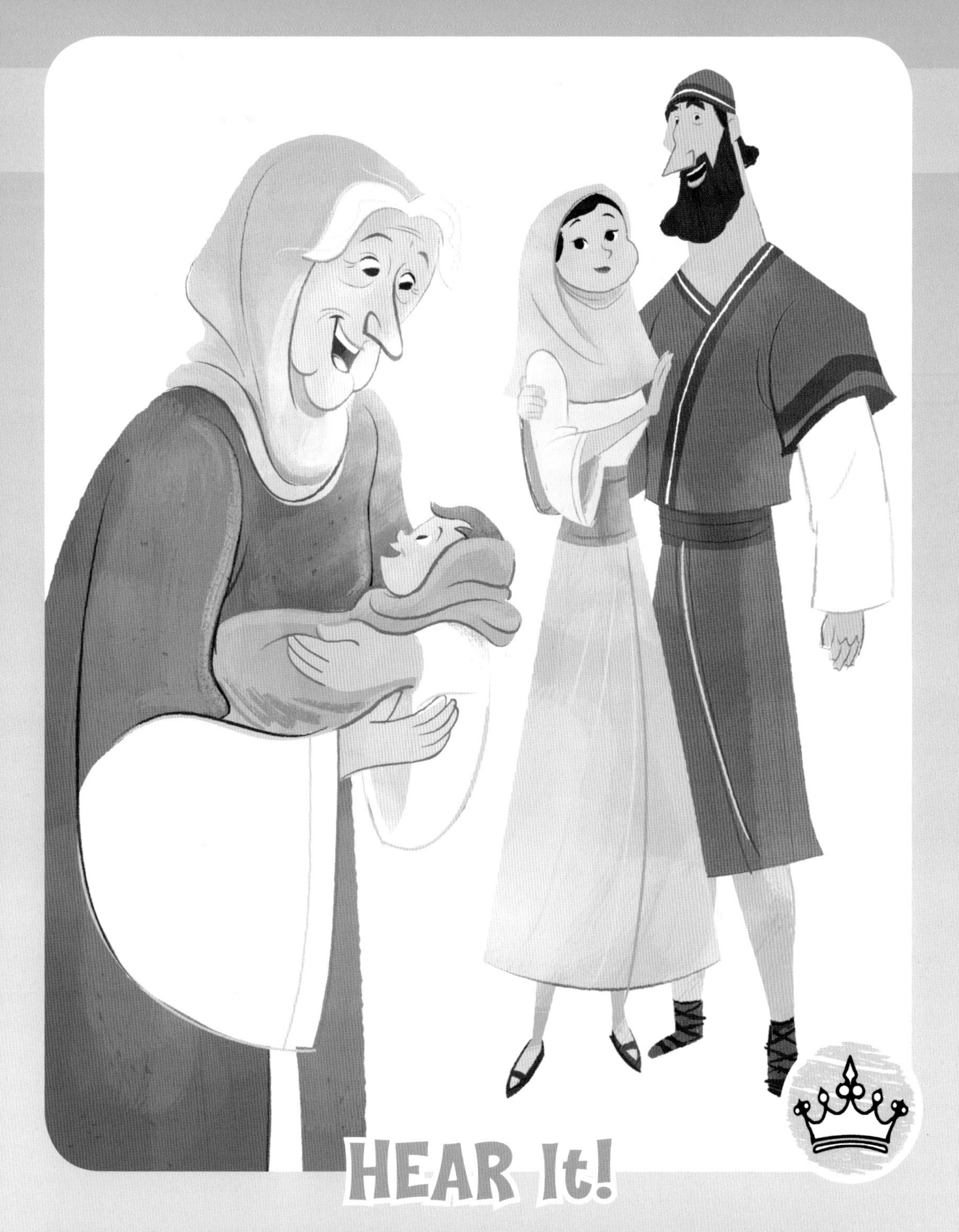

HEAR It!

Ruth was from Moab, but she married an Israelite. When her husband died, though, Ruth chose to go back to Israel with her mother-in-law, Naomi. She chose to follow God and His people. So God blessed Ruth with a new husband and a son!

Week 18

READ It!

Psalm 147:3
Deuteronomy 10:19
Matthew 25:34-40

WATCH It!

CHRIST Connection

Boaz was a family redeemer. That means he would help his close relatives who were in trouble. Boaz cared for Ruth and Naomi because their husbands had died. In a similar way, Jesus is our Redeemer. We need help because we sin. Jesus bought our salvation for us by taking our punishment when He died on the cross.

This week, look around you for someone who seems lonely. Maybe it's a new girl at school like Monique or a quiet boy on your soccer team. Reach out to him or her. Ask questions about where she moved from or where he learned to play soccer. Learn about his or her life, and share about your life too.

BIG PICTURE Questions

- Why do we need Jesus to be our Redeemer?
- Why do you think Jesus offers the same love to every single person?
- Are there any people in your life who don't seem to have many friends? Do you believe they are as valuable as the most popular kids you can think of?

Dear GOD,

Thank You for sending Jesus for everyone, not just people who seem to be important. Thank You for showing us through this story that You have made all people to have value. Help us see the world in the same way Your Son Jesus did and to show His love to those around us.

Week 19

Stand Up, Speak Up

Mason tapped the boy in front of him in the lunch line. "What are you eating for lunch, Toad?" Some kids had started calling Todd Smith "Toad" because of his funny voice and his recent outbreak of acne. Plus, he was really short.

"I can't hear you, Toad. Lasagna or chicken? Oh, wait. Maybe you have to eat flies and gnats!" The kids nearby chuckled.

In line behind Mason, Penelope's face grew hot. She knew it was wrong for him to be teasing Todd. She knew she could either stay silent or speak up. Penelope took a deep breath. "Stop that," she said.

Mason turned around. "What did you say?"

Penelope stood up taller. "Stop teasing him."

Mason narrowed his eyes. "Why should I?"

"Because he isn't ugly. God just made us all different. And He loves all of us."

Mason rolled his eyes. "I doubt that," he said.

Penelope stood her ground. "Well you can believe it or not. But it's true."

At recess, Todd came up to Penelope. "Thanks for what you said earlier," he said.

Penelope nodded. After a moment, she added, "Wanna swing?" Todd smiled and slid into the swing beside her.

Have you ever had to make a choice like Penelope, between speaking up or staying silent? God's servants sometimes have to say hard things, things other people don't want to hear.

Samuel was one of God's servants. God told Samuel to give the priest Eli a hard message. Samuel was afraid to speak up, much like the way Penelope was afraid to stand up to Mason, and like the way we can be afraid to tell others what God is like. We are afraid to say hard things because we fear other people. In our fear, we forget that God is with us! We forget that His truth is the best thing for everyone. When we stay silent, we don't give others an opportunity to trust God in that moment. When we speak up, we offer them a chance to know God more and love Him.

HEAR It!

Hannah prayed for a son, and God blessed her with Samuel. Hannah gave Samuel back to the Lord, to serve Him all his life. One night, while Samuel was still a boy, God called to him. Though he was young, Samuel was already becoming a messenger of God!

Week 19

READ It!

Psalm 71:8, Ephesians 4:15, Galatians 1:10-12

CHRIST Connection

Samuel used God's words to tell the people what God is like. John 1:1 says that Jesus is the Word. Jesus showed the world what God is like, and He told people to turn away from their sin. Jesus ultimately freed people from the power of sin by dying on the cross and rising again.

With your family, memorize Luke 12:11–12 this week. Then when the time comes for you to speak the truth, you can remember God's promise to give you the words you need.

BiG PiCTURE Questions

- Think about a time you wished someone had stood up for you. What do you wish they had said? What truth about God could they have spoken?
- Have you ever shared God's truth with someone else? If not, what keeps you from speaking up? If so, did the person believe you, or did he or she reject you and treat you worse?
- The Bible says our job is not to convince other people of the truth. Our job is to share God's message about Jesus and show others what God is like. Does that sound scary to you? Or does it sound exciting?

Dear GOD,

Thank You for reminding us that sometimes it will be hard to speak up for what is right. Sometimes we will be afraid to tell others what You are like. But help us be bold and courageous. Help us put our faith in You. May we be the kind of people who want to please You more than we want to please other people.

Week 20

What's Inside Matters Most

Cole slowly scanned his pile of birthday presents. *What was that huge box in the back?* Based on the wrapping paper, Cole knew it was from his parents. *Maybe it's a remote-controlled helicopter!* he thought.

Once everyone was in the room, Cole ran over to the large box, ripped off the paper, and found . . . a shelving unit.

"For organizing your closet," his mom explained.

"Thanks," Cole muttered, his heart sinking a bit.

Cole opened the rest of his presents before his dad handed him a small box. It was as light as air. Inside, he found a gift card.

"To contribute to your helicopter fund," his dad said with a wink.

Cole smiled and said, "Thanks, Dad."

Cole thought he could guess the importance of his presents based on their size. But looks can be deceiving. What was outside was far less impressive than what was inside.

When God sent Samuel to the house of Jesse to find the next king, Samuel thought God would pick Eliab, the oldest son. But God chose David, the youngest. "You can only see what is on the outside," God said to Samuel, "but I can see the heart."

Later on, when David wanted to fight Goliath, no one thought David could beat him. Goliath was almost ten feet tall, and David was just a boy. But inside David's heart was an unshakeable faith in God. Although David was smaller, younger, and less experienced, David trusted God, and God helped him defeat Goliath.

The Bible tells us that Jesus' appearance wasn't anything out of the ordinary, but His heart was even more impressive than David's. There wasn't an ounce of sin or rebellion in it. When it came time for Jesus to battle our greatest enemies—sin and death—He trusted God completely. He gave up His life and rose from the dead to prove that He had won the battle for our souls.

Humans will always care a lot about appearances. But God cares most about what's in your heart. Put your faith in Him, and He will do amazing things through you.

HEAR It!

The Philistines had a mighty warrior named Goliath. He was nine feet, nine inches tall! None of the Israelites wanted to fight him, but David—who was only a boy—said he would fight him. David knew that God would defeat Goliath for him—and He did!

READ It!

Psalm 51:10, Luke 6:45, Ephesians 3:14-21

WATCH It!

CHRIST Connection

The Israelites were up against their toughest enemies, the Philistines. They didn't stand a chance against Goliath, the mighty Philistine warrior. God gave David power to defeat Goliath. David reminds us of Jesus, who came to save us from our greatest enemies: sin and death. When we look to Jesus, the ultimate hero, He gives us salvation and eternal life.

Think about one word for something you have been paying more attention to than God lately. Write that word on a large piece of paper, and hang it up in your room. Every time you walk by it, ask God to make Himself more important to you than that thing.

BIG PICTURE Questions

- Is it comforting to know God sees your heart *all the time*? Why or why not?
- Read Isaiah 53:2–3. What does this passage say about Jesus' appearance? Read 2 Corinthians 5:21. What do we know about Jesus' heart?
- Why was Jesus' death enough to save us from sin and death and give us eternal life?

Dear GOD,

Thank You for showing us that You are more concerned with what is going on in our hearts than anything else. You know that every choice we make and every word we say depends on what's happening in our hearts. Help us understand that when we sin against You, it is because we do not trust You. Strengthen our hearts so we can live in a way that honors You. Remind us that when we give our hearts to You, You won't let us down.

Week 21

Wanted: Wisdom

What is wisdom? Take a moment to answer these true-or-false questions to find out if you would make the wise choice.

(T/F) It is wise to put your hand on a hot stove.

(T/F) It is wise to study the Bible regularly.

(T/F) It is wise to turn in your homework.

(T/F) It is wise to brush your teeth only once a week.

It was easy to determine if these were wise choices or not. But some decisions are not as clear-cut. Let's say your birthday is coming up. You'll have to decide if you should invite the whole class or just a couple of close friends to your party. Neither decision is wrong, but based on your circumstances, one decision might be wiser than the other.

Solomon knew he would have to make some tough decisions as king, so he asked God for wisdom. He wanted God's help determining what was best. After all, Solomon was only human. His knowledge was limited, and he was a sinner. But God is omniscient—which means He knows everything—and there is no sin in Him.

The Bible says, "The fear of the LORD is the beginning of wisdom" (Psalm 111:10). This doesn't mean we fear God like we would fear a lion or shark. The "fear of the Lord" is more like the "awe of the Lord." It's not a feeling of terror, but rather a feeling of worship.

When we are in awe of the Lord, we want to get wisdom from Him. We want to know what He has to say because we believe He knows what's best. And guess what? The Bible tells us when we ask for wisdom in faith, God gives it to us generously (James 1:5).

Think back to the wisdom quiz. When you were younger, you might not have known all those answers. The truth is, the older we get, the more we can grow in wisdom, or the more we can ignore it. Do you want to grow in wisdom? If so, pray for it, look for it, and ask God to be your source for wisdom.

HEAR IT!

God told King Solomon to ask for anything he wanted. Now, Solomon could have asked for great riches or power, but instead he asked for the wisdom to lead God's people. Because of Solomon's humble request, God gave him wisdom—and great riches and power too!

Week 21

READ It!

Psalm 111:10, Proverbs 1:1-7, James 3:13

WATCH It!

CHRIST Connection

King Solomon could have asked for earthly treasures, but he asked for wisdom to lead God's people. God created people to do His will. Jesus provided the ultimate example by completely trusting God with His life. Jesus gave up His own life to die on the cross for our sins so that God could bring us back to Himself.

Choose one of the topics below. Using a Bible concordance (printed or online), research what the Bible says about the topic. As you continue to study the Bible, you will grow in wisdom.

- Working hard
- Generosity
- Memorizing Scripture
- Kindness

BIG PICTURE Questions

- Do you remember making an unwise decision? What happened that makes you say it was unwise?
- Is there something going on in your life that you would rather not hear God's opinion about? Something you'd rather keep to yourself and figure out on your own? How can you get God's help with this problem?
- Proverbs 14:12 says, "There is a way that seems right to a man, but its end is the way to death." How can we know for sure if something is right or not?

Dear GOD,

Thank You for making Yourself knowable to us through Your Word and Your Holy Spirit. Thank You for giving us wisdom when we ask for it. Reveal to us any unwise decisions we have made, and help us choose wisdom instead. Thank You for Jesus, who demonstrated perfect wisdom. He obeyed You every moment of His life and died so our sins could be forgiven and we could know You too.

Week 22

Turn to God

Think of the meanest person you know. Is it hard for you to believe God loves that person? If God asked you to tell that person about Him, would you have a hard time obeying?

When God commanded Jonah to tell the Ninevites about Him, Jonah had a hard time obeying. The Ninevites were an evil people who did not obey God's laws. But they had not been given a chance to turn from their sins. God wanted to offer them that chance through Jonah. He wanted Jonah to tell the Ninevites: "You will be destroyed unless you turn from your evil ways and turn to Me." But Jonah wouldn't do it. He didn't think the Ninevites deserved God's mercy. So Jonah disobeyed and ran away from God.

While Jesus was on earth, He delivered God's same message to the people. He said, "Turn from your sin and turn to God. Then you will be saved." All kinds of people listened to Jesus' message and followed Him: men and women, rich and poor, young and old, good and evil. Jesus saved people you and I might not think deserve God's mercy. The Bible tells us even the criminal hanging on the cross next to Jesus believed in Him and was saved.

When Jonah was in the belly of the fish, he realized that it wasn't just the Ninevites who were sinful. He was sinful too. He had disobeyed God and run away, but God had shown him mercy by sending the fish to save him. When the fish spat Jonah back out, Jonah went to the Ninevites to deliver God's message. They listened and were saved.

When you and I don't think certain people deserve God's mercy, we (like Jonah) are forgetting that we are sinful too. We are forgetting that God's message of love is for everyone—even the "meanest" person you know. No person is so mean or so evil that God could not save him. God wants all people to turn from their sins, turn to Him, and experience His love.

HEAR It!

God told Jonah to go and warn Nineveh, but Jonah didn't want to give those people another chance. So he tried to run away from God—but he ended up in the belly of a fish for three days! Once again, God told Jonah to go to Nineveh. This time, Jonah went!

Week
22

READ It!

Romans 3:23, Romans 5:8,
2 Peter 3:9

WATCH It!

CHRIST Connection

God displayed His mercy and grace by forgiving the people of Nineveh when they repented of their sin. God showed His love to the rest of the world by sending His Son, Jesus, to die on the cross. God saves those who trust in Jesus and repent of their sin, and He sends them out, like Jonah, with the good news of salvation.

Write down the name of one person you want to tell about God this week. Then make a plan. What will you say about God?

- Is there a sin you have committed that you have never confessed to God because you think it's too big for Him to forgive?
- Is it hard for you to believe that even the meanest people in the world can be saved through Jesus?
- What does the word *mercy* mean? If you don't know, look it up in a dictionary. Talk about how God has shown us mercy.

Dear GOD,

Thank You for the Bible, which shows us what You are like. Thank You for giving Jonah and the Ninevites the chance to turn from their sins and turn to You. Thank You that we can do the same today because of Jesus. Show us if there is sin in our hearts we need to turn away from and ask forgiveness for.

Week 23

Making Hard Choices

April stared at her quiz. She only knew half of the answers. Marci, who sat next to April, was the smartest girl in class. Glancing over at Marci's paper would be easy as a wink. April chewed the eraser on the top of her pencil. Her dad would be furious if she failed this quiz. He had told her to study, but she had stayed up painting instead. April weighed her options: cheat and get an A on the quiz, or keep her eyes on her paper and fail.

If you were April, what would you do?

Shadrach, Meshach, and Abednego were in an even worse situation than April. They had two options: worship the king by bowing to his statue, or refuse to bow and be thrown into the fiery furnace. Shadrach, Meshach, and Abednego knew they would die in the fire if God did not rescue them. But they went in anyway. These three men had made tough decisions like this before (see Daniel 1), because they loved God more than anything, including their very lives.

When Jesus was on earth, He had an even more difficult decision to make. He could obey God the Father and die on the cross for our sin, or He could disobey and keep on living. Jesus gave up His life and died on the cross because He loved God the Father more than His very life. Jesus also knew that after His death, He would rise again and bring salvation to the world!

All of us will face hard choices at some point in our lives. We'll have to decide if doing the right thing is worth the difficult consequences. Although our consequence probably won't be a fiery furnace, it could be something like a failing grade, as in April's case. When the tough choices hit us, we can remember Jesus, who chose to give up His life, even though it meant dying on the cross. We can ask Him for help to make the right choice and for strength to handle what comes next.

HEAR It!

King Nebuchadnezzar ordered everyone to fall down and worship his golden statue. But Shadrach, Meshach, and Abednego knew that only God should be worshiped. And they knew that the Lord God would take care of them—even in the fiery flames of a furnace!

Week 23

Isaiah 43:2, Psalm 40:4, Matthew 10:26-31

WATCH It!

CHRIST Connection

Only God could rescue Shadrach, Meshach, and Abednego from the fire. Jesus is the only One who can save us from our sin. Jesus' sacrifice on the cross provided the way for us to be rescued and have eternal life.

Using a tape measure and sidewalk chalk, draw a line that is ten feet long on a driveway or sidewalk. (You can also do the same thing use masking tape inside!) Now imagine eight more of those lines added onto the line you drew. This was the height of King Nebuchadnezzar's statue! All along your ten-foot line, write words that describe the one true God who deserves our worship. These can be adjectives, like *good* or *holy*. These can also be words of thanks explaining what God has done for you.

BIG PICTURE Questions

- Are you surprised that Shadrach, Meshach, and Abednego were willing to die rather than bow down to the statue? What excuses could they have made for choosing to go ahead and bow to the statue?
- Imagine you are Shadrach, Meshach, or Abednego. You are standing in the fire, and it isn't burning you. What would you think? What would you do?
- Can you think of something that is the right thing to do, but really hard to do? What excuses could you come up with for *not* doing what is right? When these excuses cross your mind, what could you do to fight against them and to do the right thing?

Dear GOD,

Forgive us when we choose the easy way instead of Your way. Give us strength to do the right thing, even when it is hard. Thank You for Jesus, who did the hardest thing any human ever had to do when He gave us His life for the sins of others. Thank You for sparing us from the punishment of hell because of what Jesus did.

Week 24

God's Law Matters Most

Miss Corrie Ten Boom lived during a dangerous time in history. The Nazis had seized control of her country, the Netherlands, and were sending her Jewish neighbors off to concentration camps, where people were starved and murdered. Putting their own lives at risk, Corrie Ten Boom and her family hid many Jews in their home. When the Nazis discovered what the Ten Booms were doing, they arrested them. They sent Corrie and her sister to a concentration camp, where Corrie's sister grew ill and died. After Corrie's release, she continued to help people whom the Nazis had hurt.

Corrie Ten Boom and her family were Christians. They believed that God's law mattered more than any man-made law. When they learned that it was illegal to help the Jews, they had a decision to make. *Should we follow God's law, or man's law?* They chose to follow God's law.

The prophet Daniel had a similar decision to make. Would he obey the law of the land and pray to King Darius? Or would he pray to God only, like he always had? Daniel chose to keep praying to God and was consequently thrown in the lions' den.

Maybe you haven't had to choose between God's law and man's law yet, but maybe you've had to choose between God and your friends. Have your friends ever pressured you to do something you knew God wouldn't want? Did you wish there was some way you could please both of them? The truth is there will be times when we cannot please both God and people. We'll have to choose between them.

Choosing God shows the world how important God is. If we ignore God when others do, we're saying, "God doesn't matter much." If we obey Him when others don't, we're saying, "God matters more than anything!"

Think back to when Daniel was thrown in the lions' den. King Darius saw God rescue Daniel from the lions. After that, King Darius believed the truth that Daniel knew all along: God is the true King. His commands matter most. We should listen to Him and obey.

HEAR It!

Praying to God was now against the law—and breaking the law meant being thrown into a lions' den! But Daniel loved God and he prayed to Him just as he always had. When Daniel was thrown into the lions' den, he trusted God to save him—and God did!

Week 24

READ It!

Ecclesiastes 12:13,
Acts 5:29, Luke 6:22,
Philippians 1:29

WATCH It!

CHRIST Connection

God showed His power to rescue Daniel from the lions, but Daniel was just a small part of a much bigger story. God ultimately rescued us from a much bigger problem—sin and death—through His Son, Jesus!

Corrie Ten Boom and Daniel chose to honor God instead of men because they knew God and loved Him. With the help of your family, make a list of ten reasons God is worth obeying.

BIG PICTURE Questions

- What do Corrie Ten Boom, Daniel, and Jesus' disciples have in common?
- If you had been Daniel, what do you think you would have done about the new law? Why?
- What can you do the next time you feel pressure from your friends to do something you know God would not want?

Dear GOD,

Thank You for Your Word. Help us to believe it is worth obeying even when no one else wants to obey it. Forgive us for choosing to please people when it means displeasing You. Help us remember that You are our good king who loves us so much, and Your commands matter most.

Week 25

The Right Place and Time

Have you ever visited a friend's house and wished you could live there instead? Or have you traveled to another city and wished your family would move there? More than that, maybe there are times you wish God had given you a different family altogether.

Esther was a Jewish girl who was born in a foreign land. Her parents died when she was young, so her cousin Mordecai raised her. When she was a teenager, Esther was summoned to the palace, where the king chose her from among many women to be the next queen. Esther, who had once been an orphan, was now the most powerful woman in Persia. God had a plan for Esther's life: she would use her influence as queen to save the Jews from their evil enemy, Haman. Although Esther had no idea why she became queen, God had an idea. In fact, He knew all along.

The Bible tells us that when and where we live is not an accident (Acts 17:26). There's a reason we are in the homes we are in, with the people we are with, at this particular time in history. All of this is part of God's plan for our lives.

And God doesn't only have a plan for our individual lives. He has a plan for all of history! That plan started before the beginning of creation; it included sending Jesus at the right time to die so He could save us from our enemies—sin and Satan. God's plan for history ends with Jesus coming back to rule over the new heaven and new earth as King of kings.

So the next time you start to wonder why you live where you do when you do, and whether or not God has a plan for you, remember that God is in charge of all of history. He has put you in the right place at the right time. Even if you don't know why at the moment, God has a reason. You might find out later, or you might not. But God knows, and we can trust Him.

HEAR It!

Esther had been chosen as queen. So when Haman plotted to kill all the Jews, she was the only one who could go to the king for help—even though it might mean her death. Would the king hold out his golden scepter to her and spare her life, as well as her people?

Week 25

READ It!

Acts 17:26, Galatians 4:4-8,

Revelation 21:1-5

CHRIST Connection

Esther spoke to the king for her people in the same way that Jesus speaks to God for us. Haman tried to kill Mordecai, but God was in control, and Haman died instead. Likewise, Satan thought he had won when Jesus died on the cross, but God raised Jesus from the dead and defeated Satan once and for all.

Make a plan with your family to reach out to some of your neighbors in a special way this week. You could make a meal for them or invite them over for dinner. You could offer to do their yard work, or make them a piece of artwork. Whatever you decide to do, work on it together.

BiG PiCTURE Questions

- Have you ever wished you lived in a different house, went to a different school, or were part of a different family?
- Talk about how your neighborhood is special. What do you love about where you live? What do you wish were different about it?
- What are some ways you can help in your neighborhood or community?

Dear GOD,

Thank You for having a plan for our lives. Help us to walk in faith and trust that plan. Forgive us when we do not. You are a good God who has given us Jesus and everything else we need. Show us how You want us to live. Help us show others Your love wherever You take us.

New Testament Devotions

Week 26

When You're Not Ready

Have you ever been given a big responsibility you didn't feel ready for? Perhaps your parents asked you to clean out the garage. Or maybe you were assigned to feed and walk your dog every day.

Mary and Joseph did not feel ready for the responsibility God gave them. Before the beginning of time, God decided Jesus would come to earth as a baby, but in order for Jesus to survive as a baby, He needed parents! God could have selected anyone to be Jesus' parents. He could have chosen a king and queen. He could have picked religious leaders, or people who had raised kids before. Instead, God chose Mary and Joseph, two poor people from a small town. They had never been parents and weren't even married yet. Were they confused about God's decision? Of course. Were they afraid of what was to come? Absolutely. But did they trust God and do what He said? Yes.

Trusting God and doing what He says is called *faith*. Mary and Joseph didn't know what being Jesus' parents would be like. But they did know one thing: God was giving them this responsibility, so He would help them do it.

God often asks us to do things we don't feel ready for. But faith doesn't mean feeling ready. It doesn't mean having all the answers. Faith doesn't even mean being excited about it. Faith means trusting God will help you as you obey Him.

Do you know that when it came time for Jesus to die, He was greatly troubled about it? So troubled, in fact, that His sweat was like drops of blood. Jesus even asked God the Father if it was possible that He not die for sinners. When the Father said no, Jesus didn't walk away. He trusted God's plan with His whole heart and obeyed by dying on the cross for us.

When you don't feel ready to do something God wants, trust Him. God's grace is enough for you (2 Corinthians 12:9). He promises to never leave you (Deuteronomy 31:6). And He is always ready to help you (John 14:6).

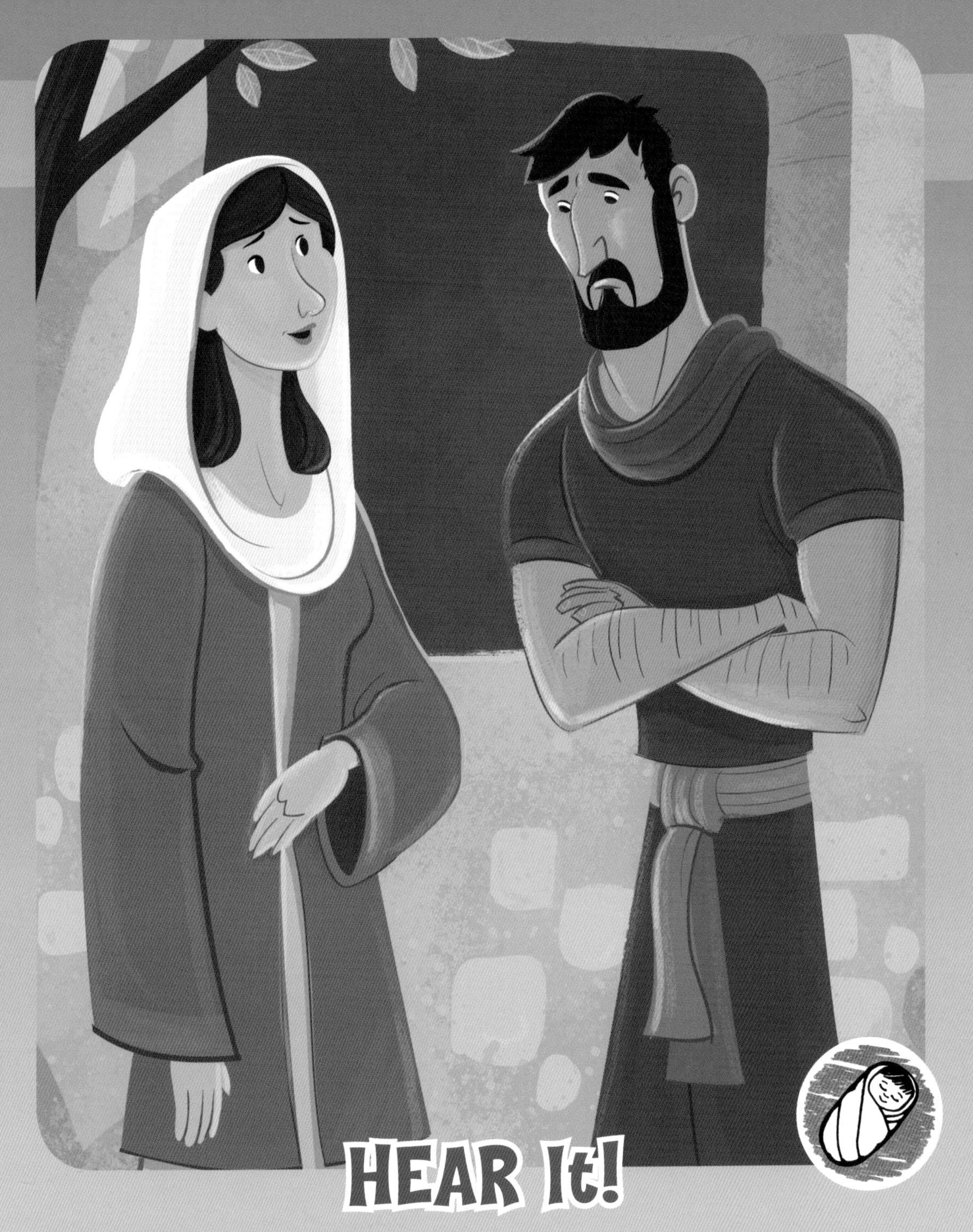

HEAR It!

Long ago, the prophet Isaiah spoke about the coming of Jesus. Now, his prophecy was about to come true! God sent His angel Gabriel to speak to both Mary and Joseph. Gabriel told them about the Child who would be born—He would be Jesus, the Son of God.

Week 26

READ It!

Luke 22:39-46, Hebrews 11:1, 2 Corinthians 12:9, Deuteronomy 31:6, John 14:6

WATCH It!

CHRIST Connection

"Therefore, the Lord Himself will give you a sign: The virgin will conceive, have a son, and name him Immanuel" (Isaiah 7:14). The baby Jesus fulfilled Isaiah's prophecy, as well as other prophecies of the coming Savior throughout the Old Testament. Through His life, death, and resurrection, Jesus fulfilled God's plan of redemption that God planned from the beginning of the world.

Draw a picture of something it would take faith for you to do. This picture might involve you giving something important to you to someone in need. It might be of you reaching out to someone at school to show God's love. Or you might draw yourself talking with a neighbor about Jesus. Share your picture with someone in your family. Ask him or her to pray that God will help you take action!

BiG PiCTURE Questions

- Why do you think God chose Mary and Joseph to be Jesus' parents?
- Have you ever felt like God was asking you to do something you didn't feel ready for? What thoughts were going through your head? What did you do?
- Why does it take faith to obey God?

Dear GOD,

Thank You for reminding us that we don't always have to feel ready to obey You. In faith, we can trust that You will give us exactly what we need each day. Thank You for Mary and Joseph, who trusted Your words and became Jesus' parents. Thank You for sending Jesus so we might have salvation through faith in Him.

Week 27

Jesus Is Special

Do you have a baby brother or sister? If so, do you remember anything about when they were first born? What do you remember most?

Think about it—God could have created humans any way He wanted. He could have made us grow on trees like apples or fall out of the sky like rain. Instead God spends nearly ten months forming and shaping us inside of our mothers. As He creates us, He chooses the color of our eyes, the shape of our noses, our personality type, and everything else about us. God makes us to reflect His image so that we can show the world some of what God is like.

When Jesus came into the world, He came the way all of us did, as a baby. This meant baby Jesus spent months growing inside His mother Mary. One day while Mary was pregnant, she visited her relative Elizabeth, who was pregnant with John. As soon as Mary entered the house, John leaped for joy because Jesus was there. *Can you believe it?* An unborn baby was worshiping God! Then because John leaped for joy, Elizabeth praised God also, and Mary rejoiced through a song of praise too!

Who was the cause of all of this praise? The unborn baby Jesus. Nobody could see Him yet. Nobody could hold Him yet. But Jesus was about to enter our world, and He was coming for a special reason. One day, Jesus would grow up to suffer and die for our sins.

This story shows us that Jesus was a special human who deserves our worship and praise. Every human God makes reflects part of His image, but Jesus is *God Himself*, reflecting every aspect of God's character. When we look to Jesus, we see exactly who God is. We know exactly what God cares about. We understand exactly how much God loves us. Jesus is not like any other human. This is why He deserved so much praise when He was an unborn baby, and it's why He deserves so much praise today.

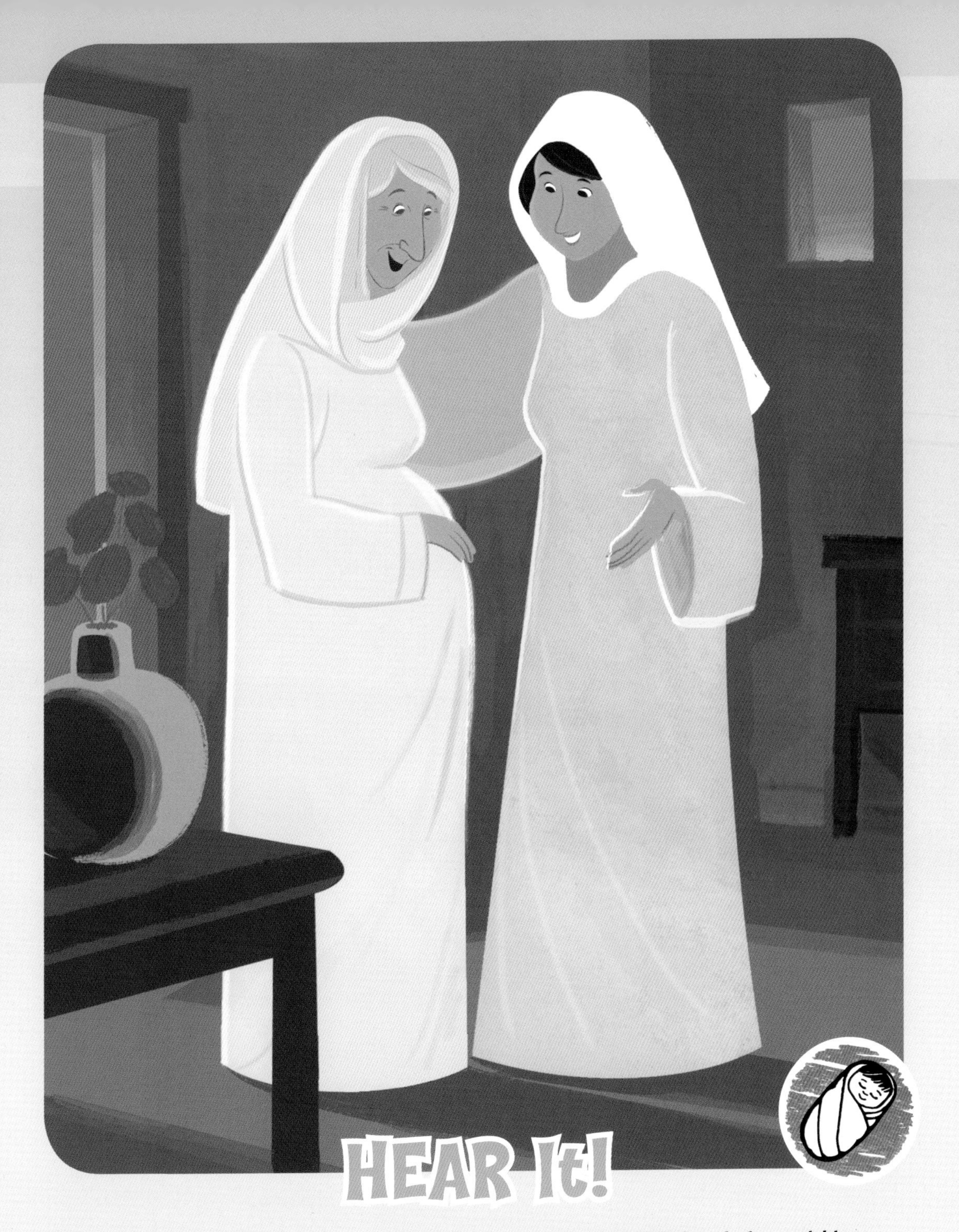

After telling Mary about the coming of Jesus, the angel Gabriel also told her about the child her cousin Elizabeth was carrying. So Mary hurried to see her cousin. When Elizabeth heard Mary's voice, the baby inside her leaped for joy!

Week 27

READ It!

Psalm 103:2, Psalm 104:33, Hebrews 1:3, John 12:45

WATCH It!

CHRIST Connection

Mary's visit to Elizabeth shows us that God was working all things together to bring about the birth of His Son Jesus to be the Savior of the world. Baby John in Elizabeth's womb leaped at the presence of his Savior in the womb of Mary. The mere presence of Jesus, even before He was born, led to rejoicing and praise by everyone there. Through praise and song they worshipped God because of Jesus.

Mary wrote a song of praise to Jesus. Write your own song of praise! If you don't want to come up with a new song, sing a song of praise with your family. Remember that you can sing this song no matter what you've done this week!

BiG PiCTURE Questions

- Do you feel guilty about something right now? What is it?
- Have you ever thought, *God doesn't like me*, because of something you did? How about *God must like me!* because of something you did? What were those things? God loves you, no matter what you've done or haven't done, and He always deserves our worship.
- What are three things you can praise God for right now?

Dear GOD,

We don't have to fix ourselves before we talk to You or worship You. We don't come to You because of the things we've done. We come to You because of what You have done for us in Jesus. Thank You for this story of John the Baptist leaping in his mother's womb, which shows us all people, no matter what they have done or haven't done, no matter how old they are, no matter what choices they have made, can worship You.

Week 28 God's Most Important Message

Lindsey's little brother Tommy came skipping over to her at the lunch table.

"I heard something important on the playground," he said.

Lindsey rolled her eyes. Tommy's friends couldn't possibly have something important to say. "Not now," Lindsey said, turning back to her best friend.

"Fine." Tommy stood up. "More for me!"

That evening, Tommy and Lindsey's parents asked them how school was. "It was great," Tommy exclaimed. "Right after school, Patrick's mom brought cake, and there was even ice cream too!"

"What?" Lindsey asked. "Why didn't you tell me?"

"I tried to," he said.

Lindsey blushed. "Oh, at lunch," she said. "Man . . . I wish I had listened!"

John the Baptist was a prophet who lived at the same time as Jesus. God gave John the Baptist an important message for the people. He said, "Get ready. Jesus is coming! Turn from your sins and be saved."

Soon Jesus came along and said, "Here I am! Turn from your sins, and come to Me. I am the one who can save you!" This is the most important message anyone will ever hear. And God invites us, once we believe it, to go out and share that message with others.

Did you know God has lots of important messages to share with His people? These messages can be found in the Bible. The Bible records everything God wanted to say to humans. It shows us the truth about God and the truth about the world. It reminds us that we are sinners who desperately need Jesus.

God gives us messages in the Bible so that we will do something about them. After all, what good is hearing a message if you don't respond to it? Imagine Lindsey had listened to Tommy's message . . . but then didn't go get some cake and ice cream. That would have been worse than if she hadn't heard the message at all! In a similar way, God's messages to us aren't just for hearing. They are for doing something about. They are also for sharing with others.

HEAR It!

Zechariah had not been able to speak since he had seen the angel in the temple. But now it was time for his son to be born. When the people asked what the boy's name should be, Zechariah wrote: "His name is John!" And instantly, Zechariah could speak again!

Week 28

READ It!

Mark 1:15, James 1:22,

Romans 10:13-15,

2 Corinthians 5:20

WATCH It!

CHRIST Connection

A long time before Jesus was born, prophets said that Jesus would come. The prophets also said another man would come first to say, "Jesus is almost here!" The people needed someone to get them ready for Jesus. John the Baptist told people to turn away from their sins because Jesus was coming to be King over the whole world.

Develop a secret code with your family. This could be a written code—where you identify certain symbols or numbers to represent letters in the alphabet—or a verbal code, like Pig Latin. Deliver messages to each other throughout the week using this code. Aren't you glad God's messages to us aren't written in code? We can read them and understand them in our own language in the Bible!

BiG PiCTURE Questions

- John the Baptist told people, "Jesus is coming!" Today we can tell people, "Jesus is coming back!" What else can you tell people about Jesus?
- Why do you think Jesus' message is the most important one anyone will ever hear?
- What is one thing you have learned recently from the Bible? After you learned it, what did you do?

Dear GOD,

Thank You for the message of Jesus. Thank You for using us to spread His message. Remind us that Your Word has many messages from You. You want to speak to us, and You want us to share what we learn with others. Thank You for giving us the Holy Spirit to teach us and to give us the courage to share what we have learned.

Week 29

God's Great Gift

Max grabbed the football jersey out of the shopping bag and held it up proudly. He had been saving his allowance up for months to purchase this particular jersey. Max folded it up nicely, set it in the box, and began cutting, folding, tucking, and taping. Soon, Max was headed out the door with a Christmas present under his arm and a smile on his face. He was off to deliver this gift to Landry, the neighborhood bully, who lived two doors down.

Does it surprise you that Max was giving his gift to a bully? If Max and Landry were best friends, this story would make sense. After all, we like to give presents to friends and people we love. As humans, we tend to care about people who care about us. But God's love is not like that. It is radically different. God even loves those who ignore Him, disrespect Him, and hate Him. The Bible says we were God's enemies, but He still loves us.

How can we be certain that God loves us? Because of the gift of Jesus! Over two thousand years ago, Jesus left heaven and came to earth as a baby. This had been God's plan all along. The day Jesus was born, I can imagine that God the Father wore the biggest smile on His face. He was so pleased to give us the gift Jesus, even though we did not deserve Him.

Think back to the story of Max and Landry. How do you imagine Landry responded when Max knocked on the door? Did he accept Max's gift? Did he tease Max for bringing it? Did he invite Max inside? The truth is, we never know how someone will respond to God's radically different love. But we do know that once we have God's love inside us, He wants us to share it with everyone.

The next time you give someone a present or open a present of your own, remember the precious gifts you have received from heaven. Remember the gift of Jesus, the gift of salvation, and the gift of God's great love. And remember that these gifts should be shared!

HEAR It!

Mary and Joseph were in Bethlehem when the time came for Jesus to be born. There were no rooms for them, so Mary had her baby in a place where animals were kept. The Son of God—the King of all heaven and earth—was wrapped in cloths and laid in a feeding trough.

Week 29

READ It!

Romans 5:6, 1 John 4:10, Matthew 18:11

WATCH It!

CHRIST Connection

The birth of Jesus was good news! Jesus was not an ordinary baby. He is God's Son, sent to earth from heaven. Jesus came into the world to save people from their sins and to be their King.

Next time it's Christmas or your birthday, share one of the gifts you receive with someone you might have a hard time loving. For example, if you get a new game, you could ask your brother or sister to play it with you. You could even loan it to him or her to play with friends. Remember how God showed us His great love: when we were His enemies, He gave us the best gift, Jesus.

BIG PICTURE Questions

- What is the most special gift you have ever received? Why was God's gift of Jesus so special?
- Is there anything we did to earn the love God showed us?
- What can you do to worship the God who sent Jesus?

Dear GOD,

Help us to remember that You love those who ignore You, disrespect You, and even hate You. Your love is greater than we could ever imagine! Thank You for teaching us to love and give like You do.

Week 30 Jealousy Versus Contentment

Gabe was in the middle of telling a funny story to a bunch of his classmates when the bell rang and Ms. Jackson directed the class to take a seat.

"Everyone, we have a new student," Ms. Jackson explained. "Please come to the front and introduce yourself, dear."

The new kid strutted to the front of the room. He was tall, and his hair was perfectly combed. He flashed a bright smile before declaring in a thick accent, "*Bonjour*. My name is Charles Dupont, and my family just moved here from France."

Excited murmurs traveled up and down the rows, and the class quickly became all ears.

Gabe shifted in his seat. *Who does this Charles think he is,* he thought, *waltzing into the school like he owns the place? This is my school, and these are my friends. He can go back to France for all I care.*

In this story, Gabe's jealousy affected the way he viewed Charles. He hated how the other kids admired Charles. Gabe wanted them to feel that way about him, and him only.

King Herod's struggle with jealousy was much greater than Gabe's. When the wise men came to Bethlehem to worship Jesus as King, Herod was outraged. *If anyone deserves these wise men's gifts, it is me!* Herod must have thought. Herod despised the very thought of Jesus, so he demanded every boy in Bethlehem under two years old be killed.

Do you ever struggle with jealousy? Jealousy says to God, "If You really loved me, You would give me what that person has." Or "If you really loved me, you wouldn't give that person what I want most!"

The opposite of jealousy is *contentment*. Contentment says to God, "I accept Your plan, because Your way is best." Herod was not content with God's plan, so he made his own evil plan to fight against it. If we reject God's plan and act on our jealousy, we become more like King Herod. If we accept God's plan and turn from our jealousy, we become more like King Jesus.

HEAR It!

The wise men followed the star for many miles to find Jesus, the King. When they found Him, they fell to the ground and worshiped Him. But not everyone wanted to worship Him. Even as a young child there were people who wanted to kill Him. But the Lord sent His angel to keep Jesus safe.

Week 30

READ It!

Proverbs 14:30,
James 3:14-16,
Philippians 4:12-13

WATCH It!

CHRIST Connection

The wise men came to worship Jesus as King. Jesus, the King who will rule forever, as God promised to King David in 2 Samuel 7. Jesus is the true King who is worthy of all our worship.

Along the top of a blank sheet of paper, write down three things you wish you had. You could list things you can buy (such as a new phone or the latest clothes) or things you can't buy (such as popularity or awesome athletic skills). Does anyone you know have those things? If so, are you jealous of him or her?

Below each word or phrase, write a prayer, asking God to help you resist the temptation to be jealous. Then write a prayer of thanks for what God has given you.

BiG PiCTURE Questions

- Compare and contrast Herod's reaction to Jesus to the wise men's response to Jesus.
- Are you jealous of anyone right now? Or have you ever been jealous in the past? How can God help us fight against jealousy?
- Why was Jesus worthy of the wise men's worship?

Dear GOD,

Thank You for using this Bible story to remind us of what can happen when we feel jealous. King Herod was jealous of Jesus because the wise men wanted to worship Jesus instead of him. But God, only You deserve our worship. You are the only one true King. As King, You know exactly what we need at all times. Help us to remember that fact when we are feeling jealous.

Week 31

Not Too Young

Callie ran up to the sign posted by the roller coaster. She turned around, stood up straight, and motioned to her older brother Kent.

Ken approached.

"Am I tall enough?" Callie asked

Kent shook his head. "Doesn't look like it," he said. Then he held his fingers about a half an inch apart. "Missed it by that much."

Callie furrowed her brow. "I'm *never* going to be able to ride that ride," she said. "Sometimes I just want to be a grown up!"

Have you ever been frustrated about being a kid? Maybe your height has kept you from riding a roller coaster like Callie. Perhaps your weight kept you from playing a certain sport. Or maybe your parents said you couldn't do something you really wanted until you were older.

Did you know that when God looks at you, He doesn't just see a kid who's too short, too small, or too young? When God looks at you, God sees a person who He wants to follow Him with his or her whole heart.

When Jesus was only twelve years old, He stayed at the temple to ask questions about God and grow in His understanding of the truth. Jesus did this because He treasured the things of God, and He cared about His relationship with God the Father more than anything else.

Even though you are still a kid, you can treasure the things of God too, starting *now*. Later in Jesus' life, He said, "Leave the children alone, and don't try to keep them from coming to Me, because the kingdom of heaven is made up of people like this" (Matthew 19:14). The Bible also says not to let anyone look down on us because we are young, but to set an example for believers in our words and actions (1 Timothy 4:12). So even though you might be too young to do certain things in this world, you are not too young to follow God and be part of His kingdom. God wants to teach you the truth, train you in wisdom, and use you mightily in His kingdom, even today!

HEAR It!

Jesus was twelve years old when He went to Jerusalem for the Passover Feast. When it was time to go back home, Jesus stayed behind, but Mary and Joseph didn't know this. When they discovered Jesus was missing, they searched everywhere for Him. They finally found Him in the temple—in His Father's house.

Week 31

READ It!

Luke 2:40, Luke 18:16,

1 Timothy 4:12, Psalm 119:9

WATCH It!

CHRIST Connection

Jesus went to the temple to worship. He is God's Son, and He came to do God's work. Jesus taught people, suffered, died on the cross for our sins, and rose from the dead so that we too can worship God.

Go through a baby book or old photos of your family. Write down all the things you have already learned to do while growing up. This will include walking, talking, eating, going to school, learning to read, and things like that. Now make future predictions about what you will learn next year, in *five* years, and in *ten* years.

Just as we grow as humans, we also grow as followers of God. As we read the Bible, pray, obey God, and learn from other believers over the years, God will teach us more about Himself. As we continue to listen, God's Spirit will mold us and shape us to make us more like Jesus.

- Do you ever think God can't really use you in His kingdom because you are so young? If you believed God could use you just as much as He can use adults, how would your involvement at church change? How would your prayers change? How would your Bible reading change?
- If you had days to talk to your church leaders like Jesus did, what questions might you ask? Could you possibly reach out and ask those questions this week?

Dear GOD,

Thank You for the example Jesus set when He was just twelve years old, in caring about His relationship with You more than anything else. Thank You for giving the Holy Spirit to all who believe in Jesus, not just to adults. Give us the courage to follow You and a desire to learn from You. Thank You for the Bible, which teaches us so much about You, and for prayer, which is our way to talk to You.

Week 32

A Special Symbol

A proper handshake is a common symbol of greeting all over the world. But did you know the way you shake someone's hand in one country might be taken the wrong way in another? In the United States, it is common to shake with one hand, but in Taiwan, you will be considered rude if you don't use both hands. And in Brazil, a firm handshake is a good sign. But in Turkey, if your grip is too strong, you will offend the other person. You must know which kind of handshake means, "Hello, nice to meet you," to start your visit off right!

Around the world, humans convey all kinds of messages through simple, symbolic actions. Handshaking, waving, bowing, hugging, saluting, and even crossing your arms communicate messages without needing any words. Can you think of any others? What do they mean?

Baptism is a symbol of a really important message. Baptism represents what God has done for us by saving us and bringing us from death to life. It also represents our turning from sin and beginning a brand-new life with God. This is why John the Baptist was confused when Jesus wanted to be baptized. Jesus had never sinned. He didn't need to turn from anything. Jesus was already living His life in a perfect relationship with God the Father. Why would Jesus want to be baptized?

Jesus was baptized so He could identify with us and set an example for us. Jesus was also baptized as a symbol of what was to come. He went into the water to represent His death and burial. He came back out of the water to represent His resurrection.

Today, when we are baptized, we are declaring this message loud and clear: "God saves us through faith in His Son who died and rose again for us." Baptism represents dying from sin and living for Jesus Christ and being part of His family, the Church.

Although all sorts of symbols represent greetings, respect, and goodbyes in different cultures around the world, there is one symbol that shows the beauty of salvation and welcomes people into the family of God—baptism!

HEAR It!

John the Baptist was baptizing people who had confessed their sins. When Jesus asked to be baptized, John knew He didn't have any sins to confess! But Jesus wanted to be baptized to show He was willing to obey God—and this pleased God very much.

Week
32

READ It!

Romans 6:4, Philippians 1:21,
Galatians 2:20

CHRIST Connection

Jesus' baptism shows us that Jesus completely obeyed God and identified with sinners by being baptized like sinners are baptized. His baptism was a symbol or sign that He would obey God and take on the punishment for the sins of the world. His baptism points to His death on the cross. He is the only One who can save us.

With your parents' help, do some Internet research on different handshakes and greetings around the world. What is the most surprising thing you discovered? Make up a new family handshake together—silly or serious, it will send the message that you are a family!

BiG PiCTURE Questions

- Have you ever witnessed a baptism? What do you remember about it?
- Imagine someone had never heard of a baptism before. How would you describe it? What would you say it means?
- Have you been baptized?

Dear GOD,

Thank You for giving us baptism so we have a way to show the world the beauty of Your salvation. Thank You, Jesus, for identifying with us and being baptized even though You didn't have to. Most importantly, thank You for what baptism represents: You rescue us from death and raise us up to new life.

Week 33

Knowing God's Word

Taylor was having a hard time focusing on his reading assignment. He couldn't stop thinking about what happened at recess. He just knew Colt had tripped him on purpose. Colt had been jealous ever since the rest of the basketball team had named Taylor all-time point guard.

Taylor winced as he slid his thumb over his scraped-up hand. He thought about the Bible verse that said, "An eye for an eye, a tooth for a tooth." *This must mean it's okay to get back at Colt,* he thought. Taylor began dreaming up ways he could sneak a bug into Colt's lunch.

It's not wise to apply a Bible verse to your life without looking at other verses in the Bible and thinking about what God was really trying to teach us. In the case of "An eye for an eye, a tooth for a tooth," God was teaching the people about justice—that if you do something sinful, you must face the consequences. He never meant it was okay for us to seek personal revenge.

When Jesus was in the desert, the Devil used Bible verses to try to trick Jesus into sinning. The Devil likes to twist God's words to mean something they were never supposed to mean. To avoid these tricks, we must know the Bible well and ask God to help us understand it. We can also talk to our parents and teachers about what the Bible means. Keep in mind the Bible is always meant to draw us closer to God, never to tempt us to sin.

Think about Taylor again. What if along with the first Bible verse, he had also remembered that Jesus said, "You have heard that it was said, An eye for an eye and a tooth for a tooth. But I tell you, don't resist an evildoer. On the contrary, if anyone slaps you on your right cheek, turn the other to him also" (Matthew 5:38–39). In this verse, we can see both parts of God's character: God's justice *and* His mercy. Colt deserved to face the consequences for what he did. But Jesus died so Colt could be forgiven of such a sin. Keeping Jesus' mercy in mind, Taylor wouldn't have plotted to put a bug in Colt's lunch. He would have forgiven Colt and loved him instead.

HEAR It!

After Jesus was baptized, He was led by the Holy Spirit into the wilderness to be tempted by the Devil. Three times, the Devil tempted Jesus. And three times, Jesus answered him with God's own Word. Jesus faced temptation just as we do, but He never gave in to sin.

Week 33

READ It!

2 Corinthians 11:14,

James 1:13-14, Psalm 119:97

WATCH It!

CHRIST Connection

Jesus was tempted, but He never sinned. Jesus is perfect and righteous. A perfect sacrifice was required to take away sin. Jesus was that perfect sacrifice. He died on the cross to free us from sin and to give us the power to say no to temptation.

Ask different family members and friends to tell you the following: their full name, their birthday, their street address, their phone number, their parents' names, and their first memory. Were they able to remember everything? Now ask them to remember all the kids in their second grade class. Could they do it? That's probably some information they haven't had to use or remember.

We can easily remember information we have memorized and use often. This is how Jesus was with the Scriptures. They came to mind easily for Him because He loved them and knew them inside and out.

BIG PICTURE Questions

- Why do you think the Devil cares about knowing the Bible? If God's enemy knows the Bible really well, do you think we should know it too?
- What is one way you could get more acquainted with your Bible?
- Have you ever read (or heard) something in the Bible you didn't understand? What can you do when that happens?

Dear GOD,

Thank You for giving us the Bible to show us what You are like. Remind us that there is a difference between knowing what's in the Bible and trusting You because of it. Thank You for Jesus, who showed us how to use Scripture and faith to fight against the Devil's temptations. Help us love Your Word more today than we did yesterday.

Week 34 Strength in Weakness

Have you ever been assigned to pick the players for a team? You probably chose the people who were the best, the strongest, or the fastest. That makes sense if you wanted to win the game! Or maybe you picked your best friends because you knew that would be fun. But you probably didn't think, *Let me choose whoever is really bad at this game* or *I'll pick whoever is hard to play with*. That wouldn't make any sense.

When Jesus came to earth, He could have picked anyone to be His disciples. He could have chosen kings, military generals, or religious leaders. Such important people would have the power to help spread the good news of Jesus as fast as possible. Instead, Jesus picked hated people like tax collectors and uneducated people like fishermen. Why would Jesus do that?

The Bible says God uses the weak things of the world to shame the strong things of the world (1 Corinthians 1:27). This is because when we are weak, God can show His power through us. When the people around us expect to see weakness but they see strength instead, they can't help but wonder, "How do you do that?" Then we can answer, "Because God is with me!"

Jesus chose these men to be His disciples because He knew how much His love would change them. The world had seen them as weak, but His love would make them strong. They would do and say things they had never done before. They would do things no one expected them to do. And everyone would know that their power came from God.

Everyone feels weak sometimes. Maybe you feel weak because of your age. Did you know God made Josiah king when he was eight years old (2 Chronicles 34:1) and God helped David kill Goliath when David was only a boy (1 Samuel 17:33)? People are surprised when young people do great things by the power of God. They wonder, "How can someone so young do something so great?" That's when kids can say, "Because God is with me. God gives me the strength."

HEAR It!

When John the Baptist was arrested, Jesus went to Galilee and began preaching the good news of God. As Jesus was walking by the sea, He saw Peter, and his brother Andrew. They were fishermen. Jesus said to them, "Follow Me, and I will teach you to fish for people!"

READ It!

Mark 2:17,
1 Corinthians 1:26-27,
2 Corinthians 12:10,
Psalm 138:3

CHRIST Connection

Jesus taught His disciples to teach others about Him. The good news about Jesus was too great not to share with the entire world! Jesus came to save people from their sin.

Write down the name of someone who you think of as "weak" in a certain way. How do you treat him or her because of that weakness? How does God see that weakness? How could you treat that person differently when you seen him or her next?

BIG PICTURE Questions

- Did you know that ten of Jesus' twelve disciples were killed because of their faith? Why do you think the disciples were willing to die for Jesus? Who gave them the strength to suffer in that way?
- Do you ever find yourself saying, "God is the one who gave me strength to do this"? If not, could it be because you are not asking God to help you where you feel weak?
- What are two areas of weakness you need God's help with? Weaknesses can be sins (like lying), struggles (like in school), or circumstances (like being poor). Don't try to deal with these things on your own. Ask God for help with them. Ask God to demonstrate His power in your life through them, however He wants to do that.

Dear GOD,

Thank You that You are strong when we feel weak. Help me remember that I don't have to be ashamed of my weaknesses, and I don't have to deal with them on my own. I can talk to You when I'm feeling weak and ask for Your help. I want You to demonstrate Your power through me. I am glad to have weaknesses if it means Your power will be shown through me.

Week 35 Bring Your Friends to Jesus

Chloe was sitting on the top of the wall, staring off into space.

Moira walked over to her. "Wanna join me on the swings?"

Chloe shook her head. "I don't feel like playing." Moira understood. She wouldn't feel like playing either if her grandmother was sick in the hospital.

That afternoon, Moira's mom asked Moira what was bothering her. "Chloe is really sad about her grandmother, and there's nothing I can do to fix it."

Moira's mom gave her a hug. "Sometimes things are too big and too painful for humans to handle. But nothing is too big or painful for Jesus. That's why when times are hard, we take our friends to Jesus."

Moira asked, "What does that mean?"

"It means we pray. In this case, you can ask Jesus to heal Chloe's grandma. He may do it, or He may not. But we can always ask! We can also ask Jesus to comfort Chloe when she's sad. Chloe's heart is hurting right now, and Jesus is the best person to help her."

Moira sat up straight. "Okay," she said, "Can we pray for Chloe together?"

Has one of your friends ever suffered like Chloe? Did you try your hardest to help him or her, but nothing seemed to work? It's because you can never be everything your friends need—you're just a human. Jesus is the only one who can meet every need we have, including our spiritual needs. Jesus can forgive our sins, give us back our hope, comfort us, give us peace, and fill our hearts with love.

The story of the paralyzed man reminds us to bring our friends to Jesus. The man's friends couldn't heal his legs, but they knew Jesus could. So they did everything within their power to get their friend to Jesus. When Jesus saw their faith, He told the paralyzed man, "Your sins are forgiven" and healed his legs. Without the faith of his friends, the paralyzed man would have never met Jesus. Because of their faith, the man met Jesus and was never the same again!

HEAR It!

Four men wanted to bring their friend to Jesus to be healed, but they couldn't even get inside the house where Jesus was. Instead of giving up, they climbed up on the roof and cut a hole in it. Then they lowered their friend through the hole—and right in front of Jesus!

Week 35

READ It!

Philippians 4:7, 19,
2 Corinthians 1:3-4,
Ephesians 1:3,
Matthew 6:31-34

WATCH It!

CHRIST Connection

The man who was paralyzed needed to be healed. Jesus knew this and did something even greater; Jesus forgave his sins, and then He healed the man. Because Jesus is God, He has the power and authority to heal and forgive. Jesus offers forgiveness to those who trust in Him.

Write down the names of a few people you want to bring to Jesus right now. Then memorize Philippians 4:19. Throughout the week, pray through the verse, replacing the word *your* with the name of each person on your list.

BiG PiCTURE Questions

- Can you think of some physical, emotional, and spiritual needs everyone has? A few answers are food (physical), love (emotional), and forgiveness (spiritual). What are some ways you can help others with their physical needs, emotional needs, and spiritual needs? What are some ways your help might not be enough?
- When something goes wrong in your own life, do you think to pray first? Or do you usually try to fix it on your own? If we are the type of people who try to fix our problems without praying, we'll also try to fix our friend's problems without praying.
- Who are some people you want to bring to Jesus right now?

Dear GOD,

Thank You for reminding us that You are the One to satisfy all of our needs. When we put our faith in You and turn from our sins, You forgive us. Then You promise to take care of us, provide for us, comfort us, strengthen us, and never take Your love away from us. Forgive us when we try to solve our own problems without coming to You, and remind us to pray for our friends when they are suffering.

Week 36

New Commands

Michael threw his backpack and himself in the back seat, while Morgan crawled in the front. "How was school today?" their mother asked.

Michael answered right away. "Awesome. I earned a Good Citizen sticker because I let Joanna go first in line."

Morgan was quiet. "What's wrong, Morgan?" her mother asked.

"I got another yellow card," Morgan whispered.

Michael rolled his eyes. "I never used to get in trouble in Miss Jones's class."

Their mother turned around to gave Michael a stern look before facing Morgan again. "What happened?"

"I spoke out of turn when the teacher said not to."

"About what?"

"I don't know."

"It's called raising your hand," Michael muttered.

"Michael." Their mother took a deep breath. "Following rules has always been easy for you. But do you know what Jesus says about rules?"

"What?" Michael was curious. He always remembered the rules, and he figured Jesus was pretty happy about it.

"Jesus gave commands like, 'Be humble. Love God more than anything. Love your enemies, and forgive everyone.' How are you doing with *those* rules?"

Michael paused to think. He loved God, but probably not more than his video games. He certainly could care less about Brendan, his enemy at school. And he hadn't forgiven Morgan for borrowing his tablet and breaking it.

"Not good," he mumbled.

"God didn't give us rules so we can be full of pride when we keep them," their mother explained. "God's commands show us how badly we need Him to change our hearts. Even kids like you, who have an easier time with class rules, still have a hard time with all of God's commands."

"Are you saying it's okay if Morgan breaks the class rules?" Michael asked.

"No. I am saying that being prideful about earning a sticker is just as sinful as disobeying her teacher. I'm saying you need God's help, just like Morgan does, and just like I do."

When Jesus was on earth, the people made a big deal about their rules. But Jesus came along and gave new commands, which were impossible to obey! The people needed changed hearts and the power of the Holy Spirit to obey them. You and I need the same thing today.

HEAR It!

When Jesus saw the crowds, He went up on the mountain, sat down, and began to teach. He taught the people many things—about how to live, about how to treat each other, and about how to love God. These teachings are called the Sermon on the Mount.

Week 36

Matthew 23:27-28,
Ezekiel 11:19,
Galatians 5:22-25

CHRIST Connection

The scribes and Pharisees looked righteous on the outside, but Jesus taught His disciples about a righteousness that comes from the inside. People who know and love Jesus have changed hearts that want to honor Jesus.

Offer to help wash the dishes this week. Be part of the washing process, and make sure to wipe the dishes completely clean.

As you wash, remember what Jesus said about the Pharisees. They looked clean on the outside, but they were still dirty on the inside. What good would it do to clean the outside of a bowl but not the inside? Would you still want to eat out of that bowl?

- Re-read the commands Jesus gave that Michael's mother listed. Which of them is the hardest for you to keep right now? Why is it hard to keep that command?
- Rule followers are people who love rules. They feel good about themselves because they are good at keeping rules. Rule breakers are people who have a hard time keeping rules. Rules tend to make them feel bad about themselves. Are you a rule follower or a rule breaker? Why do you say so? Jesus said both rule followers and rule breakers need Him.
- Why do you think Jesus gave new commands? What did He want the people to understand?

Dear GOD,

You do not love rule followers more than You love rule breakers. You love us all so much that You sent Jesus to die for us. Forgive us when we think we don't need Jesus. Forgive us when we are full of pride for keeping the rules. Forgive us when we put ourselves down for breaking the rules. Change our hearts. Help us live by faith in Jesus and the power of Your Spirit.

Week 37 God Grows the Seeds We Plant

How does a plant start? With a tiny seed. But where did that seed come from? Another plant just like it! This is how the plant world works. Once a plant blooms, it produces more seeds so more plants just like it will grow.

The kingdom of God grows in a similar way. The seed of the good news of Jesus is planted in someone's heart. That person grows in their love for God and goes out to spread the good news so that more people might receive it and grow in their love for God too.

However, Jesus reminded us in a parable that when a farmer sows his seeds, some seeds do not fall on good soil. When it comes to the good news of Jesus, this means that not all people who hear about Jesus will grow in their love for Him. Some will ignore the good news completely, others will believe it only while it's easy to believe, and others will end up loving the things of this world more than they love God.

This parable teaches us that just because we have heard the good news of Jesus doesn't mean we believe it. Just like a seed can fall on bad soil and not grow, many people will hear about Jesus, but their love for God won't grow. How can you tell if your love for God is growing? You can ask yourself, *Do I want to hear God's words and obey them? Do I want to turn from my sins and ask God for forgiveness? Do I want to show others God's love? Do I want to talk about Jesus?*

This parable also reminds us not to worry about how people respond when we share the good news of Jesus. Just like a farmer has no control over which seeds will sprout into healthy plants, we have no control over how people will respond to hearing about Jesus. We can only pray and hope that they receive the truth, grow in their love for God, and go out and spread the good news of Jesus themselves!

HEAR It!

Jesus told a parable about a sower and his seeds. The seed is God's Word and the sower is the person who shares it. The seed is important and the sower is important, but the ground is also important. God's Word will only grow in hearts that are honest and good.

Week 37

READ It!

Mark 16:15, Matthew 10:13-15,
1 Corinthians 3:6-7,
Revelation 7:10

WATCH It!

CHRIST Connection

Not everyone believes the truth about Jesus. Some don't understand it, some believe in Jesus for selfish reasons, and some only want part of Jesus because they love other things more. But those who hear the gospel and understand who Jesus is will become like Jesus and share His good news with others.

Buy some seeds to grow inside your house or in your backyard. Plant three of the same seeds in different kinds of soil. Place them in the sunlight, and water them as often as the instructions say. Watch and record what happens—does one grow faster than the others?

Remember that God only asks that we spread the seeds of the good news. He is the one who will grow the plant.

- Who is the one who designed how a plant would grow? No matter how hard a farmer tries, does he actually have control over a plant growing?
- What do you think "the good news of Jesus" means? How would you explain it to someone?
- Have you ever tried to tell anyone about Jesus? How did he or she respond?

Dear GOD,

You could have spread the good news of Jesus however You wanted, but You chose to spread it through us. Thank You for the reminder that good news about Jesus is worth sharing. Forgive us when we don't believe that. Give us the courage to tell others about Jesus, and grant us the words to say.

Week 38

Peace in the Storm

Have you ever been in a terrible storm? What made it so terrible—the wind? the lightning? Did you panic?

Storms build when hot air and cool air come together and then create unstable air. If there is moisture in that unstable air, clouds appear and rain falls. If the raindrops inside the cloud freeze and collide, the whole cloud can become electrically charged, and lighting might flash!

Storms are common on the Sea of Galilee because cool air comes down from the surrounding mountains and warm air rises up from the sea. Strong winds also come off a nearby plateau called the Golan Heights, causing waves up to ten feet tall.

Many of Jesus' disciples were fishermen who were familiar with the Sea of Galilee and its frequent storms. But the storm that arose when Jesus was with them was worse than what the disciples were used to. In fact, it was so terrifying, they were sure they were going to die.

Where was Jesus while this storm was raging and everyone else was panicking? Fast asleep! It might as well have been a sunny, breezy afternoon. This peace Jesus experienced obviously did not come from His surroundings. It came from within. It came from His perfect relationship with God the Father. Jesus knew God had all things under control. And when Jesus stood up to speak to the wind and waves, He knew they would obey Him. Even creation knows who Jesus is: the one and only Son of God.

The Bible says when things are "stormy" in our lives, we can experience the same calm Jesus did. It's called "the peace that passes understanding" (Philippians 4:7). We can have peace when it seems like we should panic. We may never be in a terrible storm like the disciples, but we might face an illness, tragedy, or heartbreak we didn't expect.

God can give us a "peace that passes understanding" because that's the peace *He* feels. Nothing in the universe is beyond God's control. When everything around us is unstable, God remains secure, and He is mightier than any storm.

HEAR It!

The storm was terrible and the disciples were terrified. They feared that their boat would sink and they would all die! Where was Jesus? Sleeping in the back of the boat! "Save us!" the disciples cried. And Jesus did—showing that He has power over all creation.

Week
38

READ It!

John 14:1, 27, John 16:33,
Colossians 3:15, 2 Timothy 1:7,
Philippians 4:7

WATCH It!

CHRIST Connection

Who is this man? Jesus' disciples knew Jesus was a good man and a good teacher. When Jesus calmed the wind and the waves, He showed His disciples that He is also God. God rules the sea and stills its waves (Psalm 89:9).

Make a tornado in a bottle. You'll need two empty two-liter bottles, lots of duct tape, and water. Fill one of the two-liter bottles about two-thirds full of water. Turn the empty bottle upside down and place it on top of the one with water, so the two bottle openings are touching. Wrap lots of duct tape around where the bottles meet.

Turn the contraption upside down so the bottle with the water in it is now on top. Hold the bottle on the bottom steady with one hand. Quickly rotate the bottle on top with the opposite hand in a clockwise motion. Watch as a "tornado" forms!

Remember that when Jesus spoke, the wind and waves obeyed. His words are more powerful than any storm.

BiG PiCTURE Questions

- What would you have thought if you saw Jesus sleeping during the storm that day?
- What would you have thought if you saw the wind and waves obey Jesus' commands?
- Is there anything happening in your life right now that you want the "peace that passes understanding" for? What is that thing?

Dear GOD,

There are many times in our lives when we feel out of control. We don't know what to do, and we panic. But You never panic. You are always in control, and You are more powerful than anything that terrifies us. We praise You for being Almighty God. Thank You for offering us "the peace that passes understanding" through Jesus.

Week 39

God Gives Us All We Need

Have you ever gone to an amusement park and waited hours to ride one ride? Even if the ride is the best one in the park, waiting in line is not much fun, is it?

One day thousands of people had gathered to be near Jesus. Many of them were sick and were eagerly waiting for Jesus to heal them. Imagine being sick and standing around thousands of other people, craning your neck to see Jesus, wondering when it would be your turn. Now imagine, on top of that, you are hungry because you haven't eaten for hours, and there is no food nearby.

Jesus' disciples knew the crowd was hungry, and they wanted to send the people away to find their own food. But Jesus knew it was best to keep the people near Him. So from five loaves of bread and two fish, Jesus made enough food to feed thousands of people!

Sometimes it's hard to wait on Jesus. For us, that might look like praying for the same thing over and over. We will be tempted to lose our faith in Jesus when waiting on Him gets hard. But think about the crowd that day. If they had grown impatient and left to find their own food, they would have missed out on the miracle! They would not have tasted the wonderful food Jesus provided.

In Matthew 6:25–26, Jesus said, "Don't worry about your life, what you will eat, or what you will drink, or about your body, what you will wear. . . . Look at the birds of the sky. They don't sow or reap or gather into barns, yet your heavenly Father feeds them. Aren't you worth more than they?"

We have all kinds of needs. Can you think of some? God knows each of your needs, and He has the power to provide for all them. Often we don't know how He's going to do it, and sometimes we don't like how long it takes. But God's way is best, and He promises to take care of us when we wait on Him.

HEAR It!

Jesus had been teaching a great crowd of people. When evening came, He told His disciples to feed the people. One boy had five small loaves and two fish, but that wouldn't feed five thousand men! But Jesus blessed the food and all the people ate—there were even leftovers!

Week 39

READ It!

Jeremiah 32:17, Psalm 73:28, John 6:35

WATCH It!

CHRIST Connection

By feeding the five thousand, Jesus provided for the physical needs of the crowd. The next day, Jesus called Himself the bread of life (John 6:35). Only Jesus is able to satisfy our souls by providing forgiveness, friendship with God, and eternal life.

Help your parents prepare a meal to take to a neighbor in need. Tell this neighbor you are providing this meal for him or her because Jesus provides us with everything we need.

BIG PICTURE Questions

- Jesus called Himself "the bread of life." What do you think He meant by this?
- How is what Jesus does for our souls *better* than what bread does for our bodies?
- Name three ways Jesus has provided for some of your needs this week. These can be physical or spiritual needs.

Dear GOD,

You are powerful and loving, and You are the only one who can give me everything I need. Help me keep bringing my needs to you! I praise You and thank You for feeding the crowd that day so long ago. You showed me that You want to take care of me and that You have the power to do it!

Week 40 Jesus Gives Hope in Death

Zach stood in the backyard staring at the gravestone he had made for his cat, Felix. His mom walked up and gave him a big hug. "I'm sorry about Felix," she whispered.

Zach was quiet for a few moments; then he mumbled, "I wish he could have lived a little longer. He was the best pet I ever had." A tear slid down Zach's cheek. He wiped it away quickly.

Zach's mom said, "It's okay to be sad, sweetheart. Jesus cried when His friend Lazarus died."

Zach looked at his mom, curious to know more. She explained, "Even though Jesus knew He would bring Lazarus back to life, He still cried about Lazarus's death."

Zach was puzzled. "Why would Jesus do that?"

"Well, God did not design life to end in death. When God first made the world, everything was perfect. There was no pain and no sickness, and Adam and Eve would never die as long as they were obedient to God."

Zach asked, "But God is so strong. Why doesn't He just make death stop?"

"As long as sin exists, death will exist too. But Jesus commanded Lazarus to come back to life to show that He is more powerful than the effects of sin. This is why people who trust in Jesus can have hope, even though we still have to deal with death."

Zach looked concerned. "But . . . will Jesus ever put an end to death, for good?"

Zach's mom smiled. "Yes, one day Jesus will return to make a new heaven and a new earth. Revelation 21:4 says He will wipe away every tear from our eyes, and there will be no more death, crying, or pain. For those who put their hope in God, everything will be even better than the way God originally made the world."

Zach breathed a sigh of relief. "Well, that makes me feel a little bit better. But I can still be sad about Felix, right?"

His mom gave him another big hug. "Absolutely, sweetheart. We can be sad together."

HEAR It!

Jesus' friend Lazarus was very sick. His sisters sent for Jesus to help him, but He didn't come until after Lazarus had been dead for four days. Jesus went to the tomb and called, "Lazarus, come out!" And Lazarus did. Jesus did this to show that He has power—even over death.

Week 40

READ It!

Isaiah 25:8, John 5:21,
Romans 8:38-39,
1 Corinthians 15:55-57

WATCH It!

CHRIST Connection

When Jesus raised Lazarus from the dead, He showed that He has power over death. Jesus said, "I am the resurrection and the life." Jesus died on the cross for our sin and rose from the dead. He gives eternal life to those who trust in Him.

Do you know someone who has experienced something sad recently, maybe a death, an illness, or a loss? Make him or her a gift, or write and send a card. Use one of the verses from “Read it!” to offer encouragement.

BIG PICTURE Questions

- What has been your experience with death? Does it make you sad or scare you?
- How is it helpful to know that Jesus cries over death too? How is it helpful to know it was never part of God’s design for life?
- When sad things happen, is it hard to believe God still loves you? Why or why not?

Dear GOD,

Thank You for showing us that it’s okay to be sad. In this world, we will have pain because things are not as they should be. Thank You for Jesus, who is more powerful than death, who died on the cross and rose again, and who will reign forever over an everlasting kingdom. Thank You that there will be an end to death one day. Until that day, help us trust in You and rely on You to comfort us when we’re sad.

Week 41

Showing Honor

Julian rang his neighbor Chris's doorbell then leaned over to pet his dog Rex.

Chris flung the door open, his eyes bright. "Hey, Julian!" he said, dropping to his knees so Rex could lick his face. "Hey, Rex! We're going to have so much fun while Julian is gone, aren't we?"

Julian smiled. He was glad Chris was watching Rex while he went on vacation. Julian knew Chris would take care of Rex as if Rex were his very own dog.

In Jesus' parable about the talents, three slaves were put in charge of some of their master's money. The first two slaves earned even more money for their master as a sign of respect. But the third slave did not respect his master like the others. He did not want to spend the time earning more money for his master, so he hid his talent in the ground and left it there.

Julian's neighbor Chris was like one of the first two slaves from Jesus' parable. Even though Rex was not his dog, Chris treated Rex with care. He petted him, fed him, walked him, and bathed him. An irresponsible dog sitter would be like the third slave from the parable. Such a sitter would ignore Rex, forget to feed him, and never take him on walks. He would think, *This isn't my dog anyway. Why should I care about him?* If Rex ever stayed with a sitter like this, Julian would be furious when he returned.

In life, God is like the master from the parable (and Julian from the story). But God doesn't just own talents or a dog. Everything in the whole universe belongs to God! This includes our money, our time, and our skills. Being like the third slave means selfishly doing whatever we want with those resources. Being like the first two slaves means asking, "What has God given me?" and "How can I use it responsibly to honor Him?" It means cherishing what God has put us in charge of so we can show Him we love Him and honor Him.

HEAR It!

A man going on a journey gave one of his slaves ten talents, another five talents, and to a third, one talent. The first two slaves used their talents wisely and earned more for their master. But the third hid his talent away. The master was angry because he didn't use what he'd been given.

Week 41

READ It!

Deuteronomy 10:12, Proverbs 3:9, 1 Corinthians 6:19-20, Colossians 3:23-24

WATCH It!

CHRIST Connection

"Well done, good and faithful servant!" Every believer, as a servant of Christ, has the task of serving God with his or her life. We eagerly wait for the day we can share in the joy of our Master. Heaven is the joy of knowing, worshiping, and enjoying Jesus forever.

This week, offer to take care of something that belongs to someone else. Do your best to honor that person well by returning it to him or her in the same condition (or in even better condition!).

BIG PICTURE Questions

- Job 41:11 says, "Everything under heaven belongs to Me." Do you ever forget that everything you have belongs to God? Why is that easy to forget? What would you do differently if you kept that in mind?
- Think about something you have trouble being responsible with. Is it your time, your skills, or the things you own? How have you struggled with responsibility in the past? Pray and ask God to help you be more responsible in the future.

Dear GOD,

Thank You for giving us everything we have. Forgive us for believing we can do whatever we want with our resources and for not honoring You with what we have. Show us how to honor You with our money, time, possessions, and skills so You will receive glory for being such a good God to us.

Week 42 The Choice: Jesus or Possessions

Is there something you treasure so much that you might cry if you lost it? You can't stand the thought of being without it.

The rich young ruler felt this way about his wealth. One day, he approached Jesus to ask about getting into heaven. But Jesus knew this man's ultimate problem was his love of his possessions. So Jesus offered him a choice: "Choose Me, or choose your wealth. Choosing Me includes selling your possessions, giving the money to the poor, and following Me. Choosing your wealth means walking away from Me but getting to keep everything you have." The Bible says the rich young ruler went away sad because he could not have both Jesus and his possessions.

All of us have a choice: Jesus over our possessions, or our possessions over Jesus. Jesus said it is impossible to equally love Him and the things we own (Matthew 6:24). The reason is they both offer us the same things: joy and satisfaction. But although the joy and satisfaction from our possessions is always temporary, Jesus fills our hearts with a true joy and satisfaction that lasts forever. That's why when we have Jesus, we can lose everything and still be content. This is something the rich young ruler did not understand, so he walked away from Jesus.

Jesus doesn't ask all of us to sell all our possessions. But He does want us to ask ourselves, "Could I lose everything I have and still be satisfied in Jesus?" For example, if you were saving for a new game and Jesus asked you to give the money to a good cause, would you be willing to do it? Or if Jesus wanted you to share something expensive with a friend who might break it, would you refuse? The answer to questions such as these shows us what we would choose in that moment: Jesus or our possessions. As you make these choices, always remember, Jesus is far better than any earthly possession, and the satisfaction of knowing Him is worth losing everything.

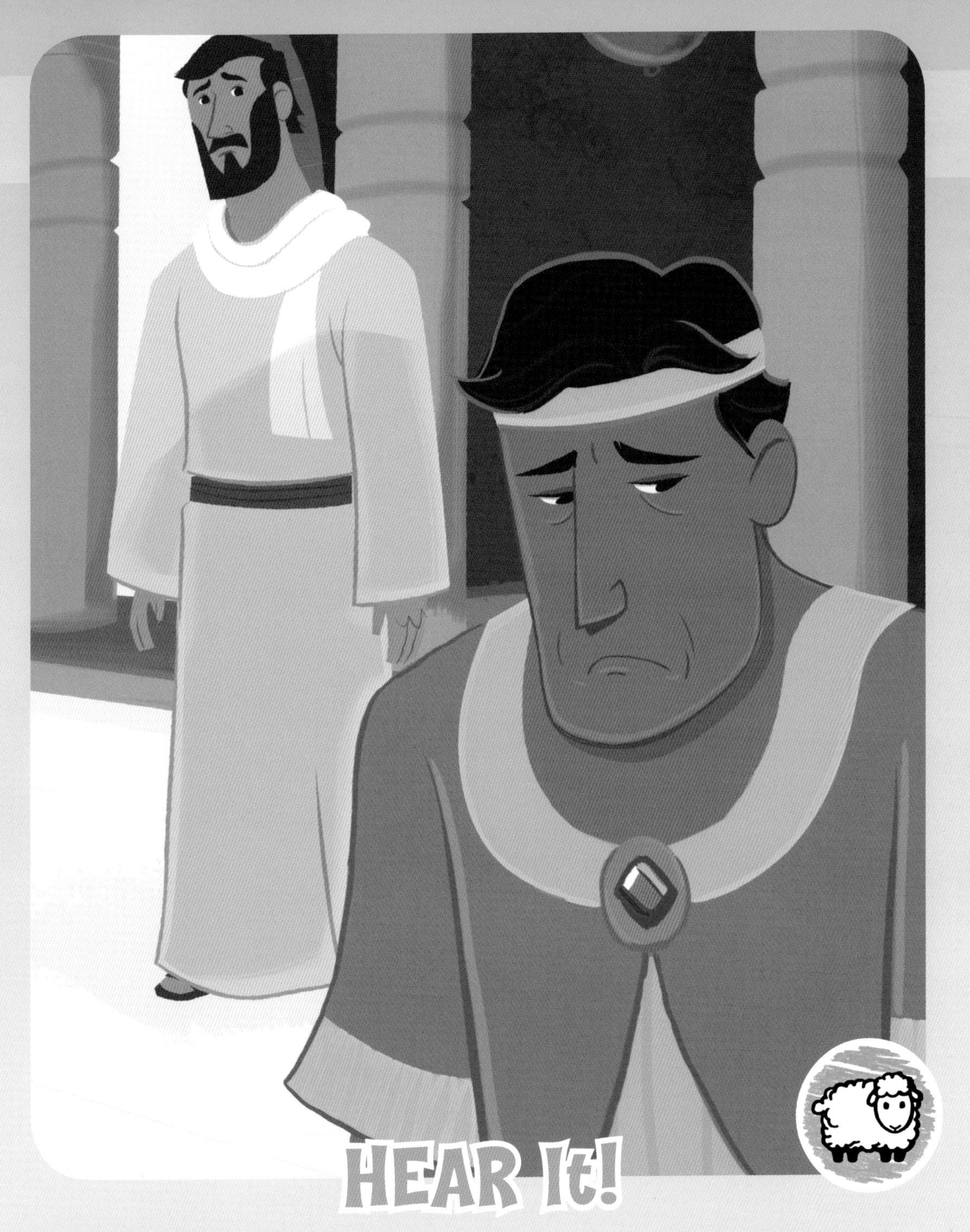

HEAR It!

A rich young ruler came to Jesus and asked what he must do to be saved. Jesus told him to give everything he owned to the poor—then he would have treasures in heaven. But the rich young ruler walked away very sad, because he loved his wealth more than he loved Jesus.

Week 42

Philippians 3:8,
Psalm 19:7-11, 73:25

CHRIST Connection

The rich young ruler loved his possessions more than he loved Jesus. Jesus asks us to be willing to give up everything and follow Him because He is ultimately the only One worth following. Jesus is better than any treasure on earth. As people who know and love Jesus, we receive eternal life.

On a sheet of paper, write down five possessions you are grateful for. Now imagine each one was taken away and not replaced. Write down how you would feel.

On the back of the paper, write down five blessings you get by following Jesus. You might include things like joy or a future home in heaven! Now, think about how this list of things can't be taken away from you like the other list can. Isn't that wonderful?

BiG PiCTURE Questions

- What are some of your favorite possessions? How do these things bring you joy and satisfaction? Do you think you will feel the same way about these possessions ten years from now? Why or why not?
- If it isn't bad for us to own possessions, what exactly is bad for us when it comes to possessions?
- Can you think of a specific time you chose the satisfaction of your possessions over following Jesus? What can you do the next time you have to make that choice?

Dear GOD,

Thank You for sending Jesus, the greatest treasure. Help us believe that following Him is far better than clinging to any possession we have. Forgive us when we choose worldly things over Jesus, and remind us that the joy of our possessions lasts only for moment, but the joy of Jesus' love lasts forever.

Week 43 The King We Did Not Expect

Cassi plopped herself down at the dinner table in a huff.

"What's wrong?" asked her mother.

"Our new principal," Cassi grumbled. "The teachers told us he would be awesome, but he's not exactly what I expected."

"What do you mean?"

"Well," Cassi said, "today the principal walked into the gym to meet us and give a big speech. If he's so awesome, I thought he'd be this really exciting guy who would make recess longer and make the teachers give us less homework. My friends and I even hoped he would announce that it was "free ice cream at lunch" day. But the only thing he's excited about is learning and getting the whole school to work together. That's boring! And he doesn't even like ice cream."

"Maybe you have to trust his plan," her mother suggested.

"Yeah," Cassi sighed. "I just wish he had a different plan."

Many Jewish people living at the time of Jesus felt like Cassi did. They expected God's promised Savior to be an earthly king, a king who would overthrow the Roman government and make them a great nation. They watched Jesus as He taught in the synagogues, performed miracles, and forgave sins. *Is Jesus God's promised king we have been waiting for?* they wondered.

When Jesus entered Jerusalem riding on a donkey, the people even worshiped Him as king. But soon, it became clear Jesus would not be the king they wanted Him to be. He had no interest in overthrowing the Romans. The people thought, *Jesus says He's the Son of God . . . but that can't possibly be!* So they demanded that He be crucified because they thought He was blaspheming against God.

Sometimes we can be a lot like these people. We love God when He's doing exactly what we expect. But as soon as God does something we don't like, we get upset. When that happens, we can remember this story about Jesus. In the end, Jesus was God's promised king; He was just the kind of king no one had ever seen! Jesus was the king who sacrificed His life so all who believe in Him could enter God's kingdom. God's promised king was far better than the earthly king the people expected. How can you worship King Jesus today?

HEAR It!

The prophet Zechariah had said the promised King would come, riding on a donkey—and Jesus did! The people covered the road with palm branches and their own robes. They praised God and shouted, "The King who comes in the name of the Lord is the blessed One."

Week 43

READ It!

Isaiah 53:1-6, 55:9,

John 18:36, 1 Timothy 1:17

WATCH It!

CHRIST Connection

During Jesus' triumphal entry, the people welcomed Him as King. Jesus was the Messiah spoken about by the prophet Zechariah: "Look, your King is coming to you; He is righteous and victorious, humble and riding on a donkey, on a colt, the foal of a donkey" (Zechariah 9:9).

Look up the following Old Testament prophecies and the corresponding verses that show Jesus fulfilled that prophecy. Jesus fulfilled many other prophecies too. If you want to find out what they are, do some research by yourself or with a family member. Share what you learn with a friend or neighbor!

He came from Bethlehem.
Old Testament—Micah 5:2
New Testament—Matthew 2:1

He would be sold for thirty pieces of silver.
Old Testament—Zechariah 11:12–13
New Testament—Matthew 26:15

He would heal the deaf and blind.
Old Testament—Isaiah 35:4–6
New Testament—Luke 7:22

He would be buried in a rich man's tomb.
Old Testament—Isaiah 53:9
New Testament—Matthew 27:57-58

BiG PiCTURE Questions

- Have you ever felt disappointed because something didn't happen like you expected it to? Did the situation turn out better or worse in the end?
- Why is it easier to praise God when things are going your way?
- When you don't understand what God is doing, what can you do to remind yourself that He still deserves your worship?

Dear GOD,

Thank You for sending Jesus to be the King we did not expect. Thank You that He is far greater than any king we could have asked for. Because of what He has done for us, we can enter into Your kingdom! Help us to remember that Your plans are always better than the plans we could make up for ourselves.

Week 44 Giving Everything We Have

Do you ever worry? What do you worry about? Often people worry about things that are out of their control. The Bible has an antidote for worry: *faith*.

The woman who gave her last two coins at the temple had much to worry about. She was a widow, which means her husband had died. Plus she was poor, so she could not buy the things she needed. Yet even in those circumstances, this woman gave her last two coins to God. This is because she knew the truth: we can lose everything in this world, but we cannot lose God. The widow demonstrated her faith in God by giving Him everything she had.

Faith is simply believing God and turning that belief into action. All throughout the Bible, we see people act in faith. They believe God is who He says He is, and they do something about it. For example, when David killed Goliath, David didn't worry about what Goliath could do to him. He focused on what God had already done for him as a shepherd, and he fought Goliath because of it. Faith says, "God is reliable. I can trust Him. I will give Him everything I have."

Worry is that feeling we get when our faith is not strong. Worry doubts God's goodness and wonders if God will take care of us. It is concerned He won't keep His promises. Worry keeps us focused on ourselves and takes our focus off of God. Worry says, "I cannot trust God to do what's best for me. So I will try to handle it myself."

All of us are bound to worry. It's part of being human. But worry can be used to bring us to God; it can remind us we need Him. Worry reinforces the fact that this world is uncertain, and the one Person we can rely on is God. So the next time worry comes, let it drive you to God. Remind yourself that God is good and trustworthy. In faith, hand your worries over to God, along with everything else you have.

HEAR It!

Jesus watched as a widow dropped two coins into the offering box. It wasn't very much. But Jesus called His disciples to Him, and said, "This poor widow has given more than all the others, because she has given everything she had."

Week 44

READ It!

John 14:1, Mark 9:24, Matthew 6:25-33, Philippians 4:6

WATCH It!

CHRIST Connection

Jesus gave up everything He had in heaven to come to earth and save us from our sins. Jesus even gave up His own life, dying on the cross in our place. When you know and love Jesus, you can serve Him as the Lord of your life and offer everything you have. God rewards those who seek Him.

Do a "trust fall" with your family. (At least one adult must be involved.) A "trust fall" is when one person stands on something and falls backwards into the arms of the people standing behind him or her. It is called a "trust fall" because by faith you have to believe that the people behind you will keep their promise and catch you.

BiG PiCTURE Questions

- Do you think you would have given your last two coins to God if you were in that widow's shoes? Why or why not?
- Think about a time you were worried and you tried to handle the situation on your own? What happened in that situation? How might putting your faith in God have made the whole situation different?
- Name two specific things that tend to cause you to worry right now. How could faith in God help you fight those worries? (Maybe you need to look up Scripture with a parent to find a promise from God to trust in today!)

Dear GOD,

Thank You for promising to provide for those who come to You in faith. Thank You for sending Jesus, who gave up everything so that we could have the most important thing, a relationship with You. When we begin to worry, draw us to You. Remind us of Your goodness, and teach us to put our faith in You.

Week 45

Old Tradition, New Meaning

Marian knelt down to gaze into the oven where her grandma's special cinnamon cake was rising. Most holidays, Marian had helped her grandma bake this cake. But Marian's family had moved last summer, far away from her grandparents, so this year, Marian's grandma wasn't with them.

When the timer rang, Marian's mom slid the cake out of the oven. "It's not the same without Grandma here," Marian said, sadly.

"I know," said Marian's mom, setting the cake on the counter. "But I've got an idea. Since we're going to keep up the tradition of baking the cake, why don't we use this time to remember and talk about all the fun times we have had with Grandma?"

Marian smiled. "Okay," she said. "I'll go first. I love how Grandma eats a whole spoonful of icing before she even puts any on the cake!"

Baking the cinnamon cake was a tradition in Marian's family, but the tradition took on a whole new meaning after her family moved. The night of the Last Supper, when Jesus ate the Passover meal with His disciples, He gave that special meal a whole new meaning too. Jesus explained that in the past, God's people ate the bread and drank the wine to remember how God had delivered them from slavery in Egypt. "But from now on, when you eat the bread, you will remember that My body was broken for you. And when you drink the wine, you will remember how My blood was spilled for you." Jesus was preparing His disciples for what He was about to do: suffer and die on the cross.

Today, taking communion—eating bread and drinking wine or juice—is a tradition for people who have put their faith in Jesus. We participate in this tradition to focus on Jesus' love for us and to remember what He did for us, including dying for our sins. Such love is always worth taking the time to remember—yesterday, today, and forever.

HEAR It!

Jesus blessed the bread and gave it to His disciples, saying, "Eat this in remembrance of Me." Then He gave thanks for the cup and gave it to them, saying, "This is My blood that establishes the covenant." Jesus' covenant would bring forgiveness to all who choose to follow Him.

Week 45

READ It!

Exodus 12:14-27,

John 6:47-51, Acts 2:42

CHRIST Connection

At the Passover, Jesus shared with the disciples His last meal before His death and resurrection. Jesus washed the disciples' feet, something a lowly servant would do. Jesus showed His love even to His enemies when He washed Judas' feet as well. As sinners, we are all enemies of God. But God proved His love for us in that while we were still sinners, Christ died for us (Romans 5:8).

Why not brainstorm ideas to start a new tradition in your family? It could be something simple like eating spaghetti on Saturday nights, or something bigger like a service project you do together every summer. Either way, this new tradition is sure to help you make great family memories!

BiG PiCTURE Questions

- What is your favorite family tradition? Why are traditions important? Do they represent something special to you?
- Can Jesus' sacrifice sometimes be easy to forget? Why do you think it is important to remember what He did for us?
- How is being rescued from the sin in our hearts even better than being rescued from slavery in Egypt?

Dear GOD,

Thank You for the new covenant in Jesus. Thank You that through His death, our sins can be forgiven and we can know and love You. Thank You, Jesus, for choosing to lay down Your life for us. Remind us of Your love when we forget.

Week 46

Honor and Love

Carter's dad marched into his room. "Mrs. Johnson said you didn't turn in any math homework last week. You lied to me, son."

"I . . ." Carter wanted to come up with a good excuse, but he couldn't. He *had* lied, plain and simple.

"So," said Carter's dad, "we need to talk about consequences. How about two weeks of no television, computer, or video games?"

Carter nodded. It was going to be a long two weeks, but he knew the punishment was only fair.

"But what if . . ." his dad paused, coming over to the bed and taking a seat beside Carter. "What if *I* give up two weeks of my entertainment electronics instead?"

"What?" Carter said in surprise.

"Well, we've been learning about Jesus' sacrifice in church, how He died for our sins and rose again. If I do this, then both you and I might understand Jesus' sacrifice a little better."

"Wow, thanks," Carter said, pausing for a moment. "But would you want me to pay you back somehow? Maybe I could mow the lawn this week?"

Carter's dad smiled. "That does sound great, son, but Jesus never demands we pay Him back for what He has done. He offers us the gift of salvation freely. We respond by accepting this gift and loving Him in return."

In this story, Carter's dad's behavior represents Jesus' honor for God the Father and His love for us. Carter's dad didn't say, "No biggie. Don't worry about the lie, son." To say that would suggest Carter's sin wasn't a problem. In the same way, Jesus agreed with God the Father that our sin was a big deal and deserved punishment.

But then, Carter's dad offered to take on the punishment his son deserved. Do you think Carter felt loved in that moment? Certainly! In a similar way, we can be convinced God loves us because Jesus died for us and rose again, offering the gift of salvation to everyone who believes.

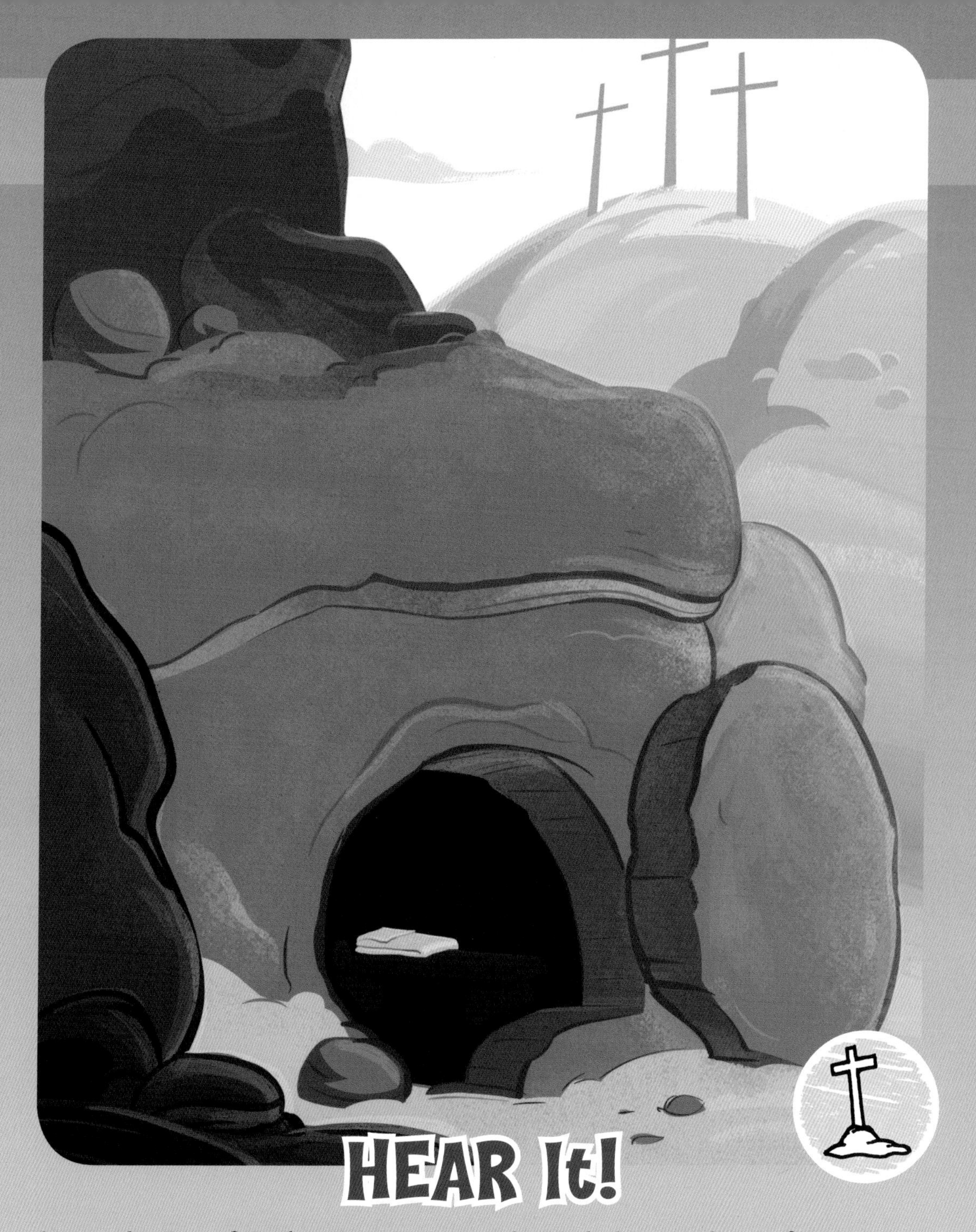

HEAR It!

Jesus, the Son of God, was innocent, yet He took the punishment for our sins. And He let Himself be killed on the cross. He was buried in a rich man's tomb, but He did not stay there. On the third day, He rose to life again—and established His kingdom, which will never end!

Week 46

READ It!

John 10:14-18, John 14:31, John 15:9

CHRIST Connection

The crucifixion and resurrection of Jesus is the center of the gospel. We deserve to die because of our sin, but Jesus died in our place. He was the blood sacrifice made once and for all for the forgiveness of sin. God was pleased with Jesus' sacrifice and raised Jesus from the dead to reign as King over all creation. We are forgiven only through Jesus (Acts 4:12).

Jesus honored the Father and showed us love when we could never pay Him back. This week, figure out a way to show love to someone without expecting anything back. You could leave a bouquet of wildflowers on the neighbor's front porch. Or clean your brother's room to surprise him. Or do something kind for a stranger who will never see you again.

BiG PiCTURE Questions

- Do you ever wish God would say, "Your sins aren't that big of a deal?" Why doesn't God say that?
- Why do you think Carter felt like he had to pay his dad back for taking on his punishment?
- Do you ever feel like you owe Jesus something for taking on the punishment for your sin? Why or why not?

Dear GOD,

Thank You for Jesus. Through His death, You showed us that You take sin seriously and that You love us so much—because He came to die in our place. There is no other love like this! We cannot understand this love, and we cannot pay You back for it, but we can accept it and then love You in return. Help us do that today and for the rest of our lives.

Week 47

Aha Moments

Have you ever heard of an *aha moment*? An aha moment is when you suddenly understand something that was unclear for a long time. Maybe this happened for you with a math concept such as fractions. You might have struggled for a while to understand numerators and denominators. But one day, someone explained them a new way, and you've understood fractions ever since.

Two of Jesus' disciples certainly had an aha moment. Jesus had recently risen from the dead, but the two disciples did not recognize Him as He joined them on their journey to Emmaus. As they walked together, Jesus taught them the truth about the Scriptures. Jesus explained how He had come to fulfill every law and prophecy in the Old Testament. He showed them that everything in the Old Testament was actually about Him! Even though the disciples had been studying the Scriptures for a while, they hadn't figured that truth out on their own. After Jesus pointed that out and revealed who He was, it all made sense! Aha!

These disciples had this aha moment with Jesus because they were *with Jesus*. They could not have figured out the truth about the Old Testament on their own. They needed Jesus' help. When it comes to aha moments with God, we need to be spending time with God in order to have them.

Sometimes we may study the Bible, go to church, and pray, but we still seem to understand very little. If you start to feel discouraged, remember the disciples needed Jesus to make the Scriptures clear, and Jesus didn't do that right away. He spent time with them on the road, *when they weren't even aware of it*, and then He made things clear later on. From this, we learn that God is with us even when it doesn't seem like it, that God reveals truth to us exactly when we need it, and that once He does, our lives will never be the same again.

HEAR It!

After He had risen, Jesus appeared to two of His disciples as they traveled along a road, but they were not allowed to recognize Him. As they walked, Jesus explained all that the Scriptures taught about Him. When they sat down to eat, Jesus gave thanks for the bread. Suddenly, they knew—this was Jesus!

Week 47

READ It!

Psalm 119:18, Ephesians 1:18, 2 Corinthians 3:16, 4:6

WATCH It!

CHRIST Connection

The Bible is all about Jesus. When Adam and Eve sinned, God began working out His plan to send Jesus to rescue people from sin (Genesis 3:15). All of the Old Testament points forward to Jesus' life, death, and resurrection—the time when Jesus would bring God's promised salvation for sinners.

Put a puzzle together by yourself. Set a timer right before you begin. Identify the moment when you know exactly where you need to put all the remaining pieces. How many pieces did you have to put together before that aha moment came? Check the timer. How long did it take before you arrived at that moment?

BiG PiCTURE Questions

- Have you ever thought you were too young to understand the Scriptures? Do you think God could reveal anything to you that He wanted? Why or why not?
- Do you ever get discouraged, thinking God isn't there because things aren't changing in your life? Name a time that has happened for you recently. (Remember that Jesus was still with the disciples, *even when they weren't aware of it*. Jesus is still with you, even when it seems like He's not.)

Dear GOD,

Thank You for being the One who reveals truth to us. Even when we don't know You are with us on the journey, You are. Help us remember this when we begin to doubt Your presence. Continue to teach us more about You and Your gospel throughout our lives.

Week 48

Believing Without Seeing

Mr. Watson stood in front of his first grade class. A pile of balloons was on the table in front of him. "I'm going to stick these balloons to the wall, without using any tape," he declared.

The kids looked back and forth at each other, confused. A boy in the front row named Derek raised his hand. "Are you gonna use glue instead?" Mr. Watson shook his head.

Marsha asked, "What about modeling clay?"

Mr. Watson said, "Nope. The balloons will stick to the wall because of something invisible called static electricity." Then Mr. Watson took a red balloon and rubbed it all over Marsha's head. Sure enough, as soon as he placed it against the wall, it stuck there.

"Whoa!" the kids cried in unison. "How did it do that?"

Mr. Watson went on to explain static electricity, a force that is invisible but still real.

After Jesus rose from the dead, He appeared to many of His disciples. One of the disciples named Thomas said, "I'll believe Jesus is alive when I see it with my own two eyes." Soon Jesus appeared to Thomas, and Thomas worshiped him. But Jesus said, "You have believed because you have seen Me. Blessed are those who have *not* seen Me and yet have believed."

The word *blessed* is another word for "truly happy." Most of us think we'd be much happier if we could see Jesus with our own two eyes. We'd know for sure He was real if we could see Him like the disciples did, face-to-face. But Jesus says we can still be truly happy, even if we cannot see Him. This is because God has sent us the Holy Spirit. The Holy Spirit comforts us, shows us our sin, gives us peace, and makes us more like Jesus. For these reasons and more, we are *blessed* when we have the Spirit. We look forward to the day when we will see Jesus face to face, but for now we are happy to have the power of the Holy Spirit in our lives.

HEAR It!

The disciples were gathered inside behind locked doors because they were afraid of the Jews. Jesus had already been killed, and they didn't want to be next. But suddenly, Jesus was there, standing right there among them. He really had risen from the dead! Jesus is alive!

Week 48

READ It!

John 14:16, 26, John 16:7,

2 Corinthians 4:18, 5:7

WATCH It!

CHRIST Connection

God made Jesus alive again! For forty days, Jesus presented Himself to at least five hundred people and proved that He is alive (1 Corinthians 15:3-8). Jesus is still alive today.

Have you ever played with magnets? Magnetism is something else we believe exists even though we can't see it. If you don't already own some magnets, purchase a set and play around with them. You'll discover that when the opposite poles are near each other, the magnets attract and fly toward each other. When the same poles are near each other, the magnets repel and flee from each other. But you can't see any of this attraction or repelling! Right now we can't see Jesus next to us either, but He is very much alive and real.

BiG PiCTURE Questions

- When Jesus appeared to His disciples, He was kind to them and gave them peace. What does this teach you about Jesus?
- Think of three things that are real even though we can't see them. These can be scientific, like static electricity, or they can be emotional, like love. How do you know for sure these things are real, even though they are invisible?
- Have you ever wished you could see Jesus face-to-face? What do you imagine that would be like?

Dear GOD,

Thank You for sending Jesus, the King who was willing to die in our place so we could have peace forever. You give all who trust in Jesus this peace through the Holy Spirit. Please point out to us when the Holy Spirit is working in our hearts, because we want to take time to thank You for that blessing.

Week 49

Jesus, Our Good King

Imagine you are out riding your bike one afternoon, and a stranger yells out at you, "Better go home and clean that bike!" You might choose to listen to him, or you might not, because he has no authority in your life as a bike expert.

But let's say you stop in at your local bicycle shop. The mechanic says, "Sounds like your bike needs some lubrication there!" You will most likely listen to what the mechanic says, because he is an authority in your life when it comes to bikes.

Before Jesus went to heaven, He said, "All authority in heaven and on earth has been given to Me. Therefore, go into all the world and preach the good news." In saying this, Jesus was reminding the disciples of who He truly was: the King of kings and Lord of lords who deserves to be worshiped all over the world.

In addition to being the King who has all authority, Jesus has promised to send us His Spirit so we will never be alone. This is why Jesus also said on that day, "I will be with you always, to the very end of the age."

Think back for a moment to the bicycle shop. Would the mechanic be a great mechanic if all he did was tell you what you needed to do? Wouldn't he be better at his job if he came alongside you and showed you how to clean your bike? Wouldn't you feel better if he told you he'd always be there to answer any questions and help you in any way?

This is what Jesus has done for us. He understands knowing what to do is not enough; we need to be reminded that He is with us. So with the authority He has been given, Jesus sends us out to tell His good news *and* He gives us the Holy Spirit to help us along the way. Jesus is truly a good and faithful king. Nothing can separate us from His love.

HEAR It!

Before Jesus went back to heaven, He gave His disciples a job to do. He said, "Go out into all the world and preach the gospel. Make disciples of all nations, and baptize them in the name of the Father and the Son and the Holy Spirit." This is called the Great Commission.

Week 49

John 20:21-22, Luke 12:12,

Romans 8:38-39

CHRIST Connection

The good news about what Jesus has done to rescue us from our sins is too great to keep to ourselves. Before Jesus went back to heaven, He gave the disciples a job to do. Jesus wants His followers to teach people everywhere about Jesus so they will trust in Him as their Lord and Savior.

Write Luke 12:12 on something small, like a piece of paper, a smooth rock, or a pink eraser. Carry this item around in your pocket all week. Whenever you put your hand in your pocket, you'll be reminded that Jesus has given the Holy Spirit to all who love Him.

BIG PICTURE Questions

- How does remembering that Jesus is king affect how you share the good news?
- How does knowing that Jesus gives us His Spirit affect how you share the good news?
- Do you believe that the good news about Jesus is worth sharing? Why or why not? When was the last time you celebrated what Jesus has done for you?

Dear JESUS,

Thank You for reminding us today of who You truly are: the King of kings and Lord of lords who deserves all worship and praise. Thank You for teaching us that when we belong to You, we never have to be alone because You give us Your Holy Spirit to help us obey Your commands. There is no one in the whole universe like You, Jesus! Help us throughout this week as we try to follow You.

Week 50

Jesus Speaks Up for Us

Mrs. Harris approached the circle of kids who had gathered excitedly. *What is going on here?* she wondered.

The kids stepped back. Billy's hands were cupped together, like he was holding something important.

"Is that another one of your pets?" Mrs. Harris asked. "I have told you before that pets aren't allowed on school property."

Billy separated his hands a bit. "Look! It's just a frog," he said. "I found it on the playground. Promise." The frog ribbited, as if on cue.

Mrs. Harris gave Billy a stern look. "I have never seen a frog on our campus before. You brought that thing from home, young man. And your mother is going to hear about it."

"Wait!" George spoke up. "It's true! I was with Billy when he found the frog by the tree." George pointed in the distance.

Mrs. Harris studied him carefully. "You know I trust you, George. You sure you're telling me the truth?"

George nodded. Mrs. Harris sighed. "Fine. Billy, release that frog where you found it. Then both of you, go wash your hands."

In this story, George spoke up on Billy's behalf. That is called is *interceding*. To *intercede* means to stand up for someone. It means to act as their voice. The Bible says when Jesus ascended to heaven, He sent the Holy Spirit to be with us and help us do God's work. But that doesn't mean Jesus is just sitting around in heaven doing nothing! Jesus lives to *intercede* for us. Jesus acts as our voice, bringing our requests to God the Father.

We cannot do this on our own without Jesus. In our sin, we can't expect God to listen to us. We can't demand to be heard. But when we trust in Jesus, He intercedes on our behalf. Now we can have confidence before God's throne. We can talk to God about anything on our minds. We can bring our requests boldly before Him.

Do you have something to speak with God about today? Ask Him or tell Him anything! Our God is eager to listen.

HEAR It!

Jesus was leaving His disciples and going back up to heaven. But He wasn't leaving them—or us—alone. Jesus promised to send the Holy Spirit to be our helper. As the disciples watched, Jesus rose up into the clouds and into heaven. And one day, He will come back again the same way.

Week 50

READ It!

Romans 8:1, 8:34,

Hebrews 4:14-16, Hebrews 7:25,

Ephesians 3:12, 6:18

WATCH It!

CHRIST Connection

Jesus left earth and returned to heaven, but He did not leave us alone. Jesus promised to send the Holy Spirit to be with us and help us do God's work. One day Jesus will return to make all things new and to rule as Lord over all.

This week, look for ways you can play the role of intercessor in your family. Look for times you can speak up for a sibling to a parent. Or deliver messages from one person to another instead of asking them to do it themselves.

What does it feel like to *intercede*? Do you feel like a servant? A helper? A friend? Remember that Jesus is all of those things for us. Right now, while Jesus is in heaven, He intercedes for us.

- How does it make you feel to know that Jesus lives to *intercede* for you? To know that He is bringing your requests before God? Does it make you want to talk to God more, or less?
- Do you ever think you can't talk to God because of the bad choices you have made? What does it feel like to stay away from God?
- What makes us confident that we can talk to God about anything?

Dear GOD,

Thank You for listening to our prayer requests because of Jesus. Thank You for giving us a perfect Savior who died for our sins so we could come to You without fear. God, You love us so much and want to have a relationship with us. Forgive us for hiding from You when we sin. Remind us that we don't have to be ashamed, but we can come to You, because we belong to Jesus!

Week 51 The Holy Spirit Honors Jesus

Samantha walked up the steps to receive the first-prize medal for the regional spelling bee. A smiling man placed the medal around her neck, then asked, "Would you like to say a few words?"

Samantha hadn't prepared any words, but the man gestured to the microphone eagerly, so Samantha stepped up to it. She cleared her throat. "This was the hardest spelling bee I've ever been in," she said, her voice shaking. "Only three people left in the final six rounds. . . But my dad made me practice the word *paraphernalia* just this morning. So I don't think I would have won without him!"

The audience chuckled.

"Actually," Samantha added. "My dad has been really great. He studied with me for hours a day. He got me a private tutor. He encouraged me when I wanted to quit."

Samantha paused to find her dad in the audience. "I wouldn't be standing here if it wasn't for him. So, Dad," Samantha grabbed her medal and held it up high. "This one's for you."

When Samantha was given the spotlight, she could have taken all the glory for herself. She could have focused on the hard work she had put in to get to where she was. Instead, Samantha shifted the focus to what her dad had done for her. Samantha wanted everyone in the audience to honor her dad because her dad deserved that honor.

This is how the Holy Spirit feels about Jesus. The Holy Spirit is always seeking to give honor and glory to Jesus. That's why when the disciples were filled with the Holy Spirit at Pentecost, they immediately started talking about Jesus.

The Holy Spirit gives glory to Jesus by changing our hearts to make us more like Him. As our hearts change, we want to love like Jesus loved and tell others about Him. If you are curious if your thoughts or actions are coming from the Holy Spirit, ask yourself the simple question, "Would this honor Jesus?" If the answer is yes, it is probably the work of the Holy Spirit inside you!

HEAR It!

Just as Jesus promised, the Holy Spirit came upon the disciples, and Peter began to preach. He said, "God has raised Jesus from the grave. Let all of Israel know that God has made Jesus—the One you crucified—both Lord and Messiah!"

Week 51

READ It!

John 7:39, 16:14, 1 John 4:2,
2 Corinthians 3:18,
1 Thessalonians 5:19

WATCH It!

CHRIST Connection

God kept His promise to send the Holy Spirit. With the Holy Spirit's help, Jesus' disciples could begin their work to share the gospel with the entire world. God gives the Holy Spirit to those who trust in Jesus as Lord and Savior. The Holy Spirit gives us power to do God's work, and He changes us to be more like Jesus.

Who is someone you could give honor to this week—maybe a teacher, a parent, a grandparent, or a coach? Identify this person, then write a note, make a gift, or serve in another way that would honor him or her. As you do this, remember what honor is. It is giving others the praise they deserve. This is what the Holy Spirit does for Jesus, because Jesus is worthy of praise!

BIG PICTURE Questions

- What do you think the difference is between the Holy Spirit and a conscience? (All people have a conscience, because we are all made in God's image. But only those who follow Jesus have the Holy Spirit.)
- Why do you think the Holy Spirit cares so much about honoring Jesus?
- Think about your life. Is there anything you are currently doing that you know for sure doesn't honor Jesus? Pray and ask God to give you the strength to fight against it. By the power of God's Spirit, you can!

Dear GOD,

Thank You for not leaving us alone, but for giving the Holy Spirit to all who believe in Jesus. Teach us to listen carefully to the Spirit as He shows us how to become more like Jesus. By the power of the Holy Spirit, help us to be brave and to share the good news about Jesus.

Week 52

Keeping the Future in Mind

Tara glanced up from her book as Principal Matthews entered the room to speak to her teacher.

"Mr. West, can we talk in the hall for a moment?"

Mr. West nodded. "Class, continue with your reading. I'll be back soon." He then followed Principal Matthews into the hall, closing the door behind him.

At first, the class remained focused on their assignment. But when two minutes went by, and still no Mr. West, some kids turned to their neighbors to chat. By the time five minutes had passed, cell phones were out, a group of kids were playing cards, and Lauren and Shawna were painting their nails. Shawna motioned for Tara to join them.

Mr. West wants us to keep reading, Tara thought, glancing over at the door. *But I want to paint my nails too!*

If you were Tara, what would you do?

The Bible tells us that one day, Jesus will come back. Just like Mr. West will not leave his class alone forever, Jesus will not remain in heaven forever. At the right time, Jesus will return in all His glory as King of kings and Lord of lords. He will defeat our enemies—including death, pain, and the Devil and his demons—for good. After that, all who love God and trust in Jesus will live with God forever in the Holy City. We know for sure this will happen; we just don't know when.

Think about the kids in Mr. West's class. Those who did whatever they wanted after Mr. West left were behaving as if they were now in charge. Those who continued reading were behaving like Mr. West was still in charge of the room, even though he had stepped out for a while.

In life, we know Jesus is still in charge and will return one day. Knowing this affects the decisions we make now. We do not ignore what Jesus has said. We do not give up when following Him gets hard. We press on, longing for the day that is coming, honoring our King who will return.

HEAR It!

The apostle John was given a vision of the day Jesus will come back. He will be riding on a white horse, and His armies will follow Him on white horses. His robes will be stained with blood. And the name written on His robe will be King of kings and Lord of lords.

Week 52

READ It!

Isaiah 65:17-19, 24-25, Matthew 24:44, Philippians 3:20, 2 Peter 3:13

WATCH It!

CHRIST Connection

Jesus promised to come back to earth soon. When Christ returns, those who trust in Jesus will be with Him and enjoy Him forever. God will undo every bad thing caused by sin—no more death, no more pain, no more tears. Jesus is making all things new.

In Revelation 19–22, the Bible describes the return of Jesus. He will come riding on a white horse and defeat His enemies. The Holy City will descend from heaven, and God will dwell among us. We are given a description of the Holy City's foundations and streets, and we are told the sun and moon will not be needed because God Himself will be the light. Choose one of these visuals to draw with art supplies. Display your drawing in your room to remind you of what will happen one day. How will you live differently now, keeping that future in mind?

BiG PiCTURE Questions

- Even though Mr. West stepped out of the room, was he still the teacher? Did he still have the authority? Why do you think some kids ignored that authority?
- Why is it sometimes hard to keep in mind that Jesus will come back? What is something you could do to remind yourself of this truth?
- What are you most looking forward to in the new heaven and new earth?

Dear JESUS,

You are King and kings and Lord of lords. You are in charge over the whole universe, and we want to live like that is true. Show us what it means to honor You while we wait for Your return. Thank You for the promise that all who love You will be with You and enjoy You forever.

978-1-5359-2220-3

978-1-5359-2221-0

Remember:

For the word of God is living and effective and sharper than any double-edged sword.—Hebrews 4:12

Read:

Read John 1:1–18. These verses remind us that God has a plan—a perfect plan of sacrifice and grace to show how much He loves us. The Bible is not just a collection of random pieces. It is one unified story—God's story of redemption. And you are a part of that story too! God wrote the Bible for us, for *you*. It is there to guide you, and each piece fits together to reveal God's big-picture plan.

Think:

1. What is your favorite Bible story? Why? What can you learn from that story to help you in *your* daily life?
2. If you could go back in time and be a part of one Bible story, which one would it be?
3. Think of someone in the Bible whom you read about in this book. How was that person's life different than yours? How was it the same?
4. Talk with your parents about some of the challenges that kids your age often deal with. It could be bullying, fighting with siblings, or not making the team. Are there people in the Bible who had similar challenges?
5. Can you think of a way God is using *your* life to teach someone else?

Do:

Create a prayer chart.

1. Go through the pages of this book and pick out three devotions whose stories seem important to you right now.
2. Find a large piece of paper or poster board, and write "Bible Story Prayer Chart" across the top.
3. Down the left side of the paper, draw a picture to represent each of your three chosen Bible stories.
4. Next to each picture, write a few words about a message you remember from that story. For example, you might write "Be brave" next to a picture you drew of Esther.
5. Draw five boxes next to each message.
6. Over the next few weeks, take the time to pray and ask God that He will help you remember these three messages. Each time you pray about one of them, check off a box.

The Bible shows us God's big-picture plan, and you are a part of it too!